THE SENSE
OF
ECUMENICAL
TRADITION

D0807963

Ion Bria

THE SENSE
OF
ECUMENICAL
TRADITION

*The ecumenical witness
and vision of the Orthodox*

WCC Publications, Geneva

Cover design: Rob Lucas

ISBN 2-8254-0966-9

© 1991 WCC Publications, World Council of Churches,
150 route de Ferney, 1211 Geneva 2, Switzerland

Printed in Switzerland

Contents

Preface

Not surprisingly, commemorations in 1988 of the fortieth anniversary of the first assembly of the World Council of Churches (WCC) have stimulated renewed consideration of how the Orthodox communion became involved in the twentieth-century ecumenical movement and the WCC.

This is not, however, a simple and straightforward historical and theological investigation. Different Orthodox churches came into the Council at different times with different expectations and have made varied contributions to it. A group of Orthodox churches related to the Ecumenical Patriarchate of Constantinople was present at the first assembly in Amsterdam and became founding members of the WCC. Other churches attending an inter-Orthodox conference in Moscow in July 1948 (just a few weeks before the assembly) decided to decline the invitation to Amsterdam. This was the first evidence at the international level that Orthodox churches differed in their approach to Christian unity. At the WCC's third assembly (New Delhi 1961) four churches from Eastern Europe were received into membership. Since then, other Orthodox churches have become members; and today all Orthodox churches, both Eastern and Oriental, belong to the WCC.

A complete account of the history of the Orthodox churches or even of their impact on the ecumenical community and the world today lies beyond the scope of this book. Nor is what follows a systematic exposition of Orthodox ecclesiology or an inter-Orthodox evaluation of the ecumenical movement.

Rather, this is an attempt first of all to explain certain positions, experiences and contributions through which the Orthodox have helped to define the ecumenical mind and vocabulary of our times and have helped to bring all churches to a new level of understanding of the tradition common to all. For centuries the Western churches, having become to a large extent confessional bodies, ignored traditions that were different from their own, while their confessional perspectives, theological methodologies and cultural realities (without which any interpretation of church history remains incomplete) passed by Eastern Christianity.

Secondly, this is an attempt to show how the Orthodox have been enriched and renewed as part of the ecumenical movement. The ecumenical evolution has offered the Orthodox a unique opportunity for openness to the outside. In this ecumenical space, the Orthodox are again finding real freedom to witness to the truth, grace and love of God in a divided world.

At a given moment in history, it was the ecumenical movement which raised the problem of the visible unity of the people of God for the life of the whole *oikoumene*. Eastern traditions played a crucial role in this. There could be no ecumenical memory without the history of twenty centuries of church life. Although the Eastern traditions are still insufficiently explored and Orthodox questions are not yet systematically communicated within the ecumenical fellowship, it is clear that the development of ecumenism depends on the "reception" of the insights of the Orthodox communion.

Ion Bria

I. The Image of Orthodoxy

There is a strange way in which Christians of other traditions comprehend Orthodoxy and indeed in which the Orthodox themselves speak about the Eastern ethos. Sacred images, solemn liturgical rhythms and a well-ordered system of symbols are used to unfold a combination of mystical and historical realities.

Efforts to describe Orthodoxy often resemble a monk trying to live outside the monastery or a prophet trying to cultivate the mystery of the living God in the dry mountains of history. Rather than a precise definition or simple descriptive explanation of Orthodoxy, there is a symbolic language that throws up a barrier to meaningful interpretation by many other confessions. The Orthodox have yet to find a true *mystagogy*, an interpretative language through which the values of their tradition can be received and appreciated by those outside.

Much of the literature which has gone into forming an image of Orthodoxy in the ecumenical arena falls short of this requirement. We must therefore focus our theological reflection in order to communicate the meaning of Orthodoxy today. We must go beyond the old habit of contrasting the values of Orthodox traditions with the weaknesses of other confessions.

At the beginning of the modern ecumenical movement, a group of outstanding theologians represented the voice of Orthodox in ecumenical meetings and conferences. They belonged to a generation that defended Orthodoxy not as a confessional or historical name, but as a continuation of the apostolic and patristic church. For them, Orthodoxy had to recover its unique role within the whole range of church history; hence their fascination with "antiquity" and the doctrine of *retour aux sources* — going back to the sources.

Several outstanding Russian Orthodox emigré theologians and religious thinkers formulated a number of ecumenical principles and convictions, particularly in ecclesiology. W.A. Visser 't Hooft identified one particularly influential aspect of Orthodoxy as these thinkers explained it:

"It was their awareness of the 'sobornost' of the church, as an integrated wholeness, which made the deepest impression on Western Christians."[1] The chapters on Orthodoxy in the standard *History of the Ecumenical Movement (1517-1948)* were written by two of these emigré theologians, Georges Florovsky and Nicholas Zernov.[2]

The major concern of this pioneer group was transposing "Eastern" theology and spirituality into a "Western" key. The style of Orthodoxy thus came to be associated with certain distinctive features and nuances formed in a particular history and context: iconography, the transfiguration of creation, a spirituality of kenosis and *theosis*, a personalist view of society and the ecclesiology of *sobornost*. From the writings of theologians like Sergius Bulgakov, Paul Evdokimov and especially Vladimir Lossky, the *Mystical Theology* (the "apophatic" way of thinking, which preserves the mystery of God) came to be taken for granted as *the* Eastern way of doing theology *par excellence*. Orthodoxy was identified with a "mode of being" and living the mystery of God. Many monographs chose subjective and mystical language to convey *The Orthodox Way*.[3] Few publications of this kind dealt with the real problems of the historical existence of the churches and the influence of non-theological factors upon them as institutions with national and social roles.

Although such a presentation was historically justified as a means of penetrating Western culture,[4] it became apparent that it was incomplete. A critique of it is now being undertaken at several theological centres, including Thessaloniki (Greece), Holy Cross (Brookline, Massachusetts, USA), St Vladimir (New York) and New Valamo (Finland). This has led to the rediscovery of such forgotten dimensions of Orthodoxy as mission, social diakonia and ethics, pastoral care, conciliarity and ecumenism. Interestingly, those who have the experience of "diaspora" are prominent among the theologians now forming such an integral picture of Orthodoxy.

Some have argued that the Orthodox church (especially in Eastern Europe) has been a church of silence, lacking freedom to implement its own values and capitulating before political powers. This assessment has come not only from Protestant churches but also from some Orthodox groups in the diaspora. Against such an approach the home churches have often taken a defensive attitude.

An entire literature has grown up around such themes as the "suffering church", "martyrs", ecclesiastical failures and compromises, a clerical church that has been unable to develop local mission freely or to dialogue with political powers. Responding to such criticism, the churches have often given an incomplete picture, withholding the voices of those who have indeed suffered. Certainly the situation of the Orthodox churches in Eastern Europe is too complex for anyone to claim to have made an adequate description of them.

The WCC has received input from the Orthodox churches on ecumenical issues, as well as on church history and theology. For more than four decades Professor Nikos Nissiotis was a brilliant interpreter of Orthodox thought in the ecumenical dialogue.[5] Through his ministry of scholarship he facilitated a contemporary "reception" of Orthodox attitudes towards and views of the ecumenical goal and way. But there have been many others as well — far too many to name here — who have made and are still making a significant contribution.

Over the last decades the WCC has published many books and studies on Orthodoxy. The Orthodox have also contributed to the reflection on the themes of WCC assemblies and to most recent ecumenical issues. There is now a new ecumenical bibliography which is an indispensable point of reference for any further studies on Orthodoxy and ecumenism.[6]

In this research the Orthodox have been prompted to go beyond the language of "witnessing to the apostolic faith of the undivided church" and to manifest the extent to which this tradition is being kept alive in specific situations, how the churches are present where the mystery of God meets people and history and how they recognize new experiences of faith in new places and in the "diaspora".

This is why an intensive attempt is now being made to find ways to communicate what the Orthodox churches are, not only as an historical model of the undivided church, but also as an empirical reality of witness and endurance.

The practice of ecumenism is more than comparing historical models. But this deeper exploration requires not only willingness in the part of the Orthodox to explore the whole truth about their tradition, but also readiness among those who want to know contemporary Orthodoxy to recognize and welcome the Orthodox contribution.

NOTES

[1] *Ecumenical Review*, VII, 4 (July 1955), 314.
[2] Vol. 1, edited by Ruth Rouse and Stephen Charles Neill (London: SPCK, 1954), pp.171-215, 645-74.
[3] The title of Kallistos Ware's book (Oxford: Mowbray, 1979); cf. V. Lossky, *The Mystical Theology of the Eastern Churches* (London: Clarke, 1957), and D. Staniloae, *Theology and the Church* (Crestwood NY: St Vladimir's, 1980).

[4] Cf. Olivier Clément, *Deux Passeurs: Vladimir Lossky et Paul Evdokimov* (Geneva: Labor et Fides, 1985).

[5] E.g., "Interpreting Orthodoxy," *Ecumenical Review*, XIV, 1 (Oct. 1961), 4-28; "The Meaning of Reception," in *Orthodox Perspectives on Baptism, Eucharist and Ministry* (Geneva: WCC, 1986), pp.47-74; "The Importance of the Trinity Doctrine," in *Le IIe Concile Oecuménique* (Chambésy: Centre Orthodoxe, 1982), pp.465-83.

[6] A brief list of these resources would include: Vasil T. Istavridis, "The Orthodox Churches in the Ecumenical Movement, 1948-68," in *A History of the Ecumenical Movement*, Vol. 2 (ed. Harold E. Fey; London: SPCK, 1970), pp.287-309; *The Orthodox Church and the Churches of the Reformation* (Geneva: WCC, 1975); Maurice Assad, ed., "Tradition and Renewal in Orthodox Education" (consultation report published by the WCC, 1977); "Orthodox Women: Their Role and Participation in the Orthodox Church" (consultation report published by WCC subunit on women, 1977); Constantin Patelos, ed., *The Orthodox Church in the Ecumenical Movement: Documents and Statements 1902-1975* (Geneva: WCC, 1978); "The Ecumenical Nature of Orthodox Witness" (consultation report published in *Ecumenical Review*, XXX, 2, April 1978); A. Sapsezian, ed., "Orthodox Theological Education for the Life and Witness of the Church" (consultation report published by PTE, 1978); Georges Tsetsis, ed., *An Orthodox Approach to Diakonia* (Geneva: WCC, 1978); Ion Bria, ed., *Martyria-Mission: The Witness of the Orthodox Churches Today* (Geneva: WCC, 1980); Ion Bria, ed., *Jesus Christ — the Life of the World* (Geneva: WCC, 1982); Todor Sabev, ed., *The Sofia Consultation: Orthodox Involvement in the WCC* (Geneva: WCC, 1982); Georges Tsetsis, ed., *Orthodox Thought: Reports of Orthodox Consultations Organized by the WCC, 1975-82* (Geneva: WCC, 1983); Ion Bria, ed., *Go Forth in Peace: Orthodox Perspectives on Mission* (Geneva: WCC, 1986); Ronald G. Roberson, *The Eastern Christian Churches* (Rome: Editioni Orientalia Christiana, 1988); Yorgo Lemopoulos, ed., *Your Will Be Done: Orthodoxy in Mission* (Geneva: WCC, 1989); Gennadios Limouris, ed., *Justice, Peace and the Integrity of Creation: Orthodox Insights* (Geneva: WCC, 1990), and *Icons: Windows on Eternity* (Geneva: WCC, 1990).

II. The Orthodox Communion

The phrase "Eastern churches" should not be understood as implying that Orthodoxy constitutes a monolithic bloc, confined to a single geographical area within Christendom. Orthodoxy is an inclusive fellowship, branching out in all continents, to all peoples and cultures.

There are different ways of mapping the Orthodox churches within global Christianity — according to the age of their organization as autocephalous entities, according to "mother" churches from which distinct missions have radiated into different regions, according to traditional cultural and theological groupings (Greeks, Slavs, Arabs), as well as churches which are now seeking fully autonomous existence which recognizes their specific cultural and spiritual ways of sharing the same faith and order.

The overview in this chapter looks at Orthodox churches in the Middle East, Orthodox churches in Central and Eastern Europe and new local churches.

A. The ancient patriarchates — Orthodoxy in the Middle East

The ecumenical participation of these venerable churches of the Middle East is important not only because they carry the most ancient Christian heritage, but also because they witness to the wounds inflicted in the past by such anti-ecumenical practices as uniatism and proselytism and because of the ecumenical relevance of their example of resistance in a situation of struggle. These modest old churches are returning to the centre of their peoples' lives and hopes.

The churches in the Middle East belong to the most ancient oriental ecclesiastical units in the world: the Patriarchates of Constantinople (Istanbul), Alexandria (Egypt), Antioch (Syria and Lebanon), Jerusalem (Jordan and the Occupied Territories), the Armenian Catholicossates of Etchmiadzin (USSR) and Cilicia (Lebanon), the Coptic Orthodox (Egypt) and the Syrian Orthodox (Syria, Beirut and India). In their organized form these churches go back to the fourth and fifth centuries. The weight of the apostolic heritage, the awareness of a long tradition and the sense of the "holy places" where the history of the New Testament was written have always played an important part in the existence and mission of these churches. To some, this "traditional Christianity" might appear rigid and outdated, but its vital role in establishing mission that has secured the continuity of Christian presence through the trials and tribulations of the ages, especially during long periods of foreign occupation and influence, should not be ignored. It symbolizes the people's loyalty to their roots.

The Ecumenical Patriarchate of Constantinople.[1] The church of Byzantium is believed to have been founded by St Andrew, brother of St Peter. It was second to Rome in the order of the ancient "pentarchy" of the five "imperial churches" established by the Ecumenical Council of Constantinople in 381 (which also completed the Orthodox creed formulated in Nicaea in 325). The symbol of the patriarchal see is the famous St Sophia church in Istanbul, erected by the Byzantine emperor Justinian. In 398 St John Chrysostom (347-407), the greatest preacher of the patristic period and author of a well-known treatise *On the Priesthood* became patriarch of Constantinople.

In 587 the Synod of Constantinople ascribed to Patriarch John IV the title "ecumenical", since the city of which he was bishop was the capital of the "ecumenical empire", the second Rome. After the great schism between Rome and Constantinople in 1054, the Ecumenical Patriarch became *primus inter pares* among the patriarchs of the Orthodox churches. This "primacy" has no doctrinal or sacramental meaning. Each local church possesses full "autocephaly" by being received and recognized by the entire Orthodox communion.

Since the ninth century, the Ecumenical Patriarchate has developed important missionary activities. Of these, the two best known were the mission to central Europe by St Cyril and St Methodius, "the Apostles to the Slavs", who devised the Cyrillic alphabet and script, and the conversion of the Rus people in Kiev in 988. The church suffered severely at the hands of the crusaders, who occupied Constantinople in 1204, and from the Turks, who captured the city in 1453. Under such adverse conditions, the church favoured the organization of autonomous and autocephalous churches in the neighbouring countries of Serbia, Romania, Bulgaria and Greece.

The Ecumenical Patriarchate today has jurisdiction over the Greek faithful in Europe, North and South America, Australia and New Zealand, the autonomous Church of Finland and the Russian diocese of

Western Europe. The Greek theologians and theological centres in diaspora play an important role in the ecumenical movement.

A leading figure in ecumenical history was the Ecumenical Patriarch Athenagoras I. His joint declaration with Pope Paul VI on December 7, 1965, lifted the mutual excommunications which dated from 1054 (see Appendix I). When Patriarch Dimitrios I visited the Ecumenical Centre in Geneva in December 1987, WCC General Secretary Emilio Castro presented him a copy of the original text of the 1920 encyclical letter from the Ecumenical Patriarchate "to all the churches of Christ everywhere", the first official church proposal for a global ecumenical instrument, which symbolizes the significant part the Orthodox churches have played in the history of the WCC.[2]

The Patriarchate of Alexandria (Egypt). This patriarchate, whose origin is traced to St Mark in A.D. 64, played an important role in the transmission of biblical texts, the history of theological thought and the defence of Orthodox doctrine at the Councils of Nicea (325) and Ephesus (431). One of its greatest theologians was St Athanasius (d. 373), biographer of St Anthony and author of *On the Incarnation*. At the time of the Reformation the see of Alexandria was occupied by several outstanding patriarchs — Meletios I Pegas, Cyril Lucaris, and Metrophanes Kritopoulos, who wrote an important *Confession of Faith* (1625).

Since the jurisdiction of Alexandria includes not only Greek and Arab communities in Egypt, but also parishes and dioceses of black African faithful in East, West and Southern Africa, the problem of indigenization of the liturgy and the promotion of indigenous clergy is a critical one for this patriarchate.[3]

The Greek Patriarchate of Antioch (Damascus). It was in Antioch that the disciples were first called Christians (Acts 11:26); and St Ignatius of Antioch (ca. 35-107), bishop and martyr, was a key figure in giving episcopal shape to the post-apostolic church. This church suffered through the Islamic advance in the seventh century and the formation of a uniate church in the eighteenth century. Its current jurisdiction covers Syria, Lebanon, Iraq and Iran. In recent decades an important Arabic-speaking diaspora has appeared in North and South America, Australia and New Zealand. Recently, the patriarchate has taken important initiatives to organize the diaspora and its ecumenical relations, and has made a concerted effort to redefine its own basic identity and vocation in the context of Syrian Christianity.[4]

The Patriarchate of Jerusalem. The first bishop of Jerusalem was St James (Acts 15:13). Before the destruction of Jerusalem by the emperor

Titus in A.D. 70, the church took refuge in Pella. The first church of the *Anastasis* (Resurrection) was dedicated around 335. In the middle of the fourth century St Cyril of Jerusalem (315-386) wrote the famous *Mystological Catechesis*. By the decision of the fourth ecumenical council the diocese of Jerusalem, which had been under the metropolitan see of Caesarea, became an independent church.

During the Byzantine period, its main preoccupation was the protection of the churches of the holy shrines: the Holy Sepulchre, Calvary, the Nativity, the Ascension and the Transfiguration. In 637 Jerusalem was conquered by the Arabs, and in 1099 by the Crusaders, who established a Latin patriarch there. In 1517 Jerusalem came under the sovereignty of the Sultan of Constantinople for 400 years. The rights of the Greek Patriarchate in the holy places were recognized by international treaties. After the end of the British mandate and the partition of Palestine, the Jordanian government promulgated a law on the patriarchate in 1958. While the patriarch is of Greek origin, there are Arabic-speaking parishes in Jerusalem, West Bank, Gaza and Jordan; hence the problem of indigenous witness and clergy.

There is a growing recognition among all churches today, reflected in many WCC statements, that the sacred shrines in Jerusalem should serve as living places of worship, belonging to the Jewish, Christian and Islamic communities who have their roots in the Holy City.[5]

"Little Vineyards of God" — The Oriental Churches

The history of the so-called imperial churches which constituted the pentarchy — Rome, Constantinople, Alexandria, Antioch, Jerusalem — is inseparable, at least for the first six centuries, from the history of the Oriental, "non-Chalcedonian" churches whose doctrines are based on the decisions of the first three ecumenical councils.[6] These churches renounced the teachings of Nestorius and the Monophysitism taught by Eutyches, but they preferred the definition promulgated by the Council of Ephesus ("one in the incarnate nature of the Logos") to the Christology of the Council of Chalcedon (451).

The Coptic Church.[7] As native Christians of Egypt, this church keeps alive the legacy of the Coptic (ancient Egyptian) language, thus feeling a particular responsibility for the study of the national culture and its ethos. According to tradition, the church was founded by St Mark the Evangelist. Its greatest ascetic was St Anthony, author of a well-known *Rule* for monastic communities, who retired to the desert of Upper Egypt in 285. After the Council of Chalcedon formulated the doctrine of the two natures

— divine and human — in the person of Christ, the Egyptian Christians joined those Orthodox who confessed only one nature — divine — in the incarnate Lord, and constituted the Coptic Church.

Over the years the Coptic Church has developed its own distinctive way of thinking and its own spirituality. Today, with about six million members, it is the largest Christian community in the Middle East. It has a large diaspora not only in Africa (Sudan, Libya, South Africa) but also in Canada, Europe and Australia. Within Egypt, its monastic centres have great spiritual influence, as do its catechetical and diaconal institutions (the church maintains the order of deaconesses).

The Armenian Apostolic Church (Etchmiadzin, Armenia).[8] This church traces its origin to the preaching of the apostles Thaddeus and Bartholomew. St Gregory the Illuminator (300-325) was the first catholicos of the Armenians. Etchmiadzin symbolizes the Armenians' national, cultural and religious unity in their homeland and abroad; and the liturgical language, classical Armenian, serves as a strong bond of unity. Apart from the See of Etchmiadzin there are two patriarchates with local jurisdiction: Jerusalem and Constantinople. Since the middle of the fifth century, the Armenians have been subject to Persians, Arabs, Turks and Russians. One and a half million Armenians were massacred by the Turkish authorities between 1915 and 1922.

Armenian Catholicossate of Cilicia (Antelias, Lebanon).[9] This was re-established and reorganized in 1930 as the spiritual centre of one part of the Armenian diaspora: dioceses and parishes in Lebanon, Syria, Cyprus, Iran, Greece and two in the USA. The emigration and deportation of the Armenians began in the tenth century. Many Armenian princes took refuge in Cilicia, where they formed an independent kingdom. From there a large number emigrated to Europe. After the fall of Constantinople (1453), Sultan Mohammad II brought in many Armenians, and an Armenian patriarchate was established there along with the Greek one.

The Ethiopian Church (Addis Ababa).[10] The church was established in the fourth century by St Frumentius and Edesius of Tyre. When the old patriarchate of Alexandria was transferred to Cairo (ca. 640), the local church became dependent on it and accepted the pre-Chalcedonian Christology. For centuries the church was under heavy pressure from the Roman popes and missionaries. In 1625 a Catholic patriarch was sent from Rome, but a proposed union with Rome was not accepted. Since 1950 the Ethiopian church has been fully autocephalous. The language used in public worship is Ge'eze.

The Syrian Patriarchate of Antioch (Damascus).[11] This patriarchate was established in the fourth century to administer the churches in the Persian Empire, Iraq and the Far East. Syrian missionaries went to Mongolia, India and China. The church suffered greatly from the Mongol invasions in the fourteenth century. The establishment of a uniate patriarchate (Syrian Catholics) diminished the force of the church. The normal liturgy is that of St James, and the liturgical language is Syriac, into which the Old Testament was translated in the first century and the New Testament in the second century.

Malankara Orthodox Syrian Church (Kottayam, Kerala, India). According to tradition, this church was founded in A.D. 52 by St Thomas the apostle, who preached the gospel in Cranganore, Kerala, and was martyred on what is now known as St Thomas Mount in Madras. The church was connected with the Roman church and associated with the Syrian church, including ownership of the temporal properties. In 1912 the patriarch Abdul Masia established a catholicate in India. However, a dissident group recognized the power of the Patriarch of Antioch in India. In 1958 the Indian Catholicos was recognized by the decision of the supreme court.[12]

* * *

These ancient churches of the Middle East have preserved the memory of the Old Testament prophets and the apostles who gathered around the name of Jesus Christ of Nazareth, born in Bethlehem, crucified in Jerusalem, by whose sacrifice all were reconciled, Jews and Gentiles alike. The history of the Christian church begins here; and it was here that baptism, eucharistic celebration and mission were established. It was in this part of the world — where scholars of the second century B.C. (in Alexandria) had made the Greek translation of the Old Testament which would later be quoted in the New Testament — that the canon of the Holy Scriptures was determined. Outstanding writers, preachers and thinkers from the great schools of theology of the Middle East elaborated the patristic tradition. The ancient centres here which convoked the seven ecumenical councils (between 325 and 787) formulated Christian doctrines and maintained pastoral responsibility.

The focal points for the authority and mission of the Middle Eastern churches are institutions that have a deep symbolic value for the community — the biblical sites, apostolic sees, patriarchates and catholicates, which recall the long history of Christianity but also give powerful expression to their pastoral and social leadership.

The link between church and nation, which led to the founding of ecclesiastical autonomy on ethnic principles, is an important feature of these churches, expressed in various forms. Most of the churches understand themselves as the real protector of their nation, people and culture. Plans to give more institutional visibility to the Christian presence in many countries (for example, by building new places of worship) demonstrate that these churches are not giving up their responsibilities in public life.[13]

The churches in Jerusalem convey an unhappy image of ecclesiastical division, whose most poignant expression is the multitude of possessors and protectors of the Holy Sepulchre. In Jordan and Israel the Orthodox mother church exists side by side with Western churches which emerged from the Crusades or foreign missionary enterprises and are not original indigenous groups (although the Latin leader is now an Arab). There is a basic human solidarity among the Arabs, both Christian and Muslim, not only in Jerusalem and the Occupied Territories but throughout Israel, Lebanon and Jordan. They constitute a strong voice pleading for a *modus vivendi* in a pluralistic society.[14]

Historical factors are decisive for the ecumenical life of the traditional churches of this region. An extremely important development is the planned reunion between the Eastern and Oriental churches (see chapter 10, pp. 99-102). A declaration of agreement to that effect was recently signed by four church leaders — the positive result of years of theological dialogue between the two families.

Reconciliation with the Roman Catholic Church raises more complicated questions, because it involves the history and attitudes of those Orthodox churches which are united with Rome — the so-called uniate or Eastern Catholic churches. These communities are clearly significant within the region, but their formation has had a deep effect on the integrity of the Orthodox churches; and the issue of the uniates remains a major and urgent subject for ecumenical examination together with the Roman Catholic Church. Another basic ecumenical issue in the Middle East is mutual recognition with the churches of Western Protestant origin, which have shown great respect for the tradition and place of the Orthodox "mother" church.

There is a need to find further expressions of unity (such as already exists among the churches in Syria and Egypt) on issues like a common date for Easter, mutual recognition of baptism, shared places of worship and parish centres, mixed marriages and Bible translation. Mutual recognition and a sense of hospitality are urgent spiritual needs.

At the heart of the matter lies the issue of how the churches perceive one another ecclesiologically: how the historical churches qualify or disqualify the more recently arrived evangelical communities and *vice-versa*. The penetration of Western confessions into the Middle East through aggressive proselytism and uniatism has created confusion. Yet in spite of divisive issues, there is no major ecumenical crisis there today. The Orthodox have conceived their mission in terms of preserving their own community in the tradition of the right faith and worship; while the diakonia of social service to which the Protestant and Catholic churches are deeply committed is a way to serve the society at large. The indigenous churches have their own specific way to practise care for the benefit of the whole society; for to keep alive the memory and express the identity of a specific nation is also a means of serving society at large.

A critical missiological and pastoral issue for the future of the churches in the Middle East is the dislocation of the mother churches as a result of emigration of their members from the region. The resulting emergence of a network of "diaspora" communities could finally erode the institutional stability of the churches which remain. Hence the need to prevent the disappearance of the "original" communities by halting the displacement of the indigenous people.

All Middle Eastern churches oppose the often ideologically rooted disregard of the rights of the Palestinian people and are ready to mobilize urgent public attention to the need to solve this problem, which is not merely political but also economic and social.

The Middle East is supremely that part of the world where the Christian community encounters Islam and Judaism with their respective communities.[15] Christians refuse to be considered as a minority or a special category of people in this context. Without losing their confessional identity or abandoning their traditional structures, the churches are promoting dialogue and better understanding with people of other faiths, living together and working for peace in the region.

The Middle East has specific vocations and special expectations to fulfill for the benefit of other regions. One example is the monastic centres of the Coptic Church, especially its network of deaconesses, which has already had a significant influence in several Balkan countries. Another is the extension of mission and pastoral care from the centres in the region to the Orthodox communities in Africa. The future of a genuine African Orthodoxy is in the hands of the Patriarchate of Alexandria, which has a long-term involvement in the indigenization of Orthodox tradition in African culture. The Coptic Orthodox Church is also active in

African solidarity and ecumenism. The role of the present church leaders is essential for taking initiatives to create a form of conciliarity whether within a single country or in the region as a whole.

B. Orthodoxy in Central and Eastern Europe — "Byzance après Byzance"

At the WCC's third assembly (New Delhi 1961), the Russian, Romanian, Bulgarian and Polish Orthodox churches joined the Council. [16] The Serbian Orthodox Church became a member in 1962; the Czechoslovakian in 1967. With the entry into the WCC of these six churches, Eastern Orthodoxy, which had been partially represented since 1948, became as a whole an organic part of the ecumenical movement. What is especially significant about this is that these churches brought into the ecumenical arena one of the most challenging Christian experiences of our century.

Concerning the admission of these churches at the New Delhi assembly, Visser 't Hooft wrote:

> Their joining must be considered as a major event in the history of the ecumenical movement. In this way a tremendous opportunity is offered to us, the opportunity to ensure that a real spiritual dialogue shall take place between the eastern churches and the churches which have their origin in the west. If we accept this opportunity, our ecumenical task will not become easier, but we shall surely be greatly enriched. In this respect the strengthening of our stakes will be especially necessary, and that all the more since we have not only to count with the ancient divergences between the Christian east and the Christian west, but also with the modern tensions between the political east and the political west. [17]

Recent developments in this region, where the largest national Orthodox churches are located and the majority of the Orthodox faithful live (about 90-95 million of a total of 110-115 million), lend new importance and interest to an analysis of the experience of the Orthodox in Central and Eastern Europe. The Orthodox churches here are highly diverse in history, cultural heritage and socio-political milieu. Theologically and culturally we can describe them in the famous words of the Romanian historian Nicolas Iorga: "Byzance après Byzance" — "Byzantium after Byzantium". In the ninth century, Patriarch Photius of Constantinople (810-895) sent two Byzantine missionaries from Salonica, St Cyril and St Methodius, to "Great Moravia" to convert Slavs, Czechs, Moravians and Poles, whom they taught in the vernacular. Through the activities of their disciples among the Slavic peoples of Bulgaria and Yugoslavia, they came to be known as "the Apostles to the Slavs". [18] The root of their entire missionary endeavour was the translation of the Bible and the Eastern liturgy into a language their converts understood. The "Church Slavonic" they created became the common vehicle of Christian culture among Orthodox Slavs.

In 1988, when the Russian Orthodox Church commemorated the millennium of the baptism of its people, it was in direct link with the Patriarchate of Constantinople. The Romanian Orthodox Church, which historically and linguistically goes back to apostolic times, was organized autonomously in the fourteenth century with the canonical assistance of the Ecumenical Patriarchate. The Georgian Orthodox Church embraces the majority of the people of a country that became Christian by the preaching of Ste Nina of Cappodocia around A.D. 330. At first dependent on the Patriarchate of Antioch, it became autocephalous in the eighth century.

While these churches identified with a national and social group in their respective countries, they also tried in different ways to emulate the model of the Byzantine synthesis. After the fall of Constantinople in 1453, this became an important element of ecclesiastical policy. The Russian church saw its position in the fifteenth and sixteenth centuries as a continuation of the great Byzantine Church and called itself "the third Rome". [19] The central vision was that of transferring "Byzance" into these regions, culturally and politically. Indeed, the modern organization of these churches as national autocephalous churches and patriarchates has echoed the famous Byzantine "symphony" between state and church — misleading now, because it was based in part on the mediaeval Christian state.

Over the past fifty years, Eastern European Orthodoxy has not shown much interest in a critical interpretation of its own history. There is a vast amount of material to be analyzed, but little of it has been collated, much less interpreted. However, one can identify several phases which constitute the historical background to the contemporary scene, of which the most determinative are:

1. The inter-Orthodox conference in Moscow in July 1948 was important because of the attention it gave to the transition to a new social system in the period after World War II. Obliged to formulate and proclaim their response to society in a new political context, the churches launched a new pastoral theology which stressed Christian responsibility to work for social justice and to oppose poverty and war.

Coming only a few weeks before the WCC's Amsterdam assembly, the Moscow conference adopted a resolution against the ecumenical movement. The division within Orthodoxy in approaching the ecumenical cause appeared clearly at the international level. The conference demonstrated that the Orthodox at this historical moment took differing points of departure into the new period, played different roles within their own nations and had different levels of theological education and ecumenical experience. In 1948 it would have been difficult to give a single description of the unity of Orthodoxy itself.

By rejecting participation in the ecumenical movement and membership in the WCC, the Orthodox churches present in Moscow declared a sort of interruption of contacts with the ecumenical community at large. This created particular problems for the churches with organized dependent communities abroad.

2. Efforts to come to terms with the new post-war social realities in the 1950s and 1960s were not soundly undertaken. The churches were pushed into accepting an institutional separation from the state, a barrier betwen faith and social science, an ideological understanding of religion and ethics and restrictive legislation on religious freedom.[20] In interpreting this context, theologians were tempted to take for granted certain ideological presuppositions which they would be reluctant to accept today: the definition of religion as a "private affair", "folk-church" as a merely sociological reality, the end of the "Constantinian era" and the validity of Marxist analysis for sociology. From the perspective of the last few years, the theological motivation given for church social ethics at the beginning of this period has many apparent limitations.[21]

By entering fully into the ecumenical movement after 1961, these Orthodox churches recognized that their experiences and struggles cannot be isolated from those of the rest of the church universal. Their life must be shared, but it must also be open for criticism and correction.

3. In the 1980s, these churches realized that they were in danger of becoming clerical institutions, out of touch with the people. Within their churches they saw not only a sense of alienation and an absence of conciliar spirit, but also a lack of knowledge and analysis. The church authorities hesitated to take initiatives regarding the agenda of the next pan-Orthodox Synod, because that would risk conflict with the people, who had a different agenda and a different spirit.

4. A major task facing Orthodox churches in Central and Eastern Europe today is to assess the dynamics of the economic and socio-

political upheaval in their part of the world — the liberating factors and positive developments, as well as new difficulties and threats. What makes the European scene move? What will influence the situation of Christianity?

Many signs indicate that Europe is at the end of an anomalous period created by the division of the continent into antagonistic political and military blocs after World War II. During the four decades of the Cold War there were always a few voices raised against the ideological and economic barriers dividing Europe; but in the late 1980s the communist systems and Stalinist dictatorships established in Eastern Europe crumbled completely. Their fall has various names: perestroika, economic restructuring, transition to a market economy, anti-communist revolution, democratization. The most vivid symbol of this is the reunification of Germany and dismantling of the Berlin Wall. Hopes are high that the spirit of permanent confrontation which characterized post-war Europe will disappear.

At the same time, there are new signs of the emergence of a common European tradition sustained by Christian values. The search for visible unity among churches, both in bilateral dialogues and in the ecumenical movement, is important for European culture and society. The ecumenical assembly on Peace with Justice, organized by the Conference of European Churches and the European Catholic bishops conferences in Basel in 1989, strengthened the churches' solidarity in a new conciliar process around European issues. The ecumenical climate in Europe is also revitalized by the concern for evangelism in many churches and by ecumenical work in translating and distributing the Bible. Another hopeful sign is the Community of Taizé, which has inspired the spiritual life and unity of young people. The admission of Greece into the European Community has raised intriguing possibilities for the penetration of the Orthodox tradition and values into Western Europe.

Above all, there is in Central and Eastern Europe a profound religious renaissance in the midst of deep secularism. After more than four decades of the terrifying rejection of religion, people hunger to be near to God, to experience the joy of being the children of God.

Both within and outside Central and Eastern Europe there is a perhaps understandable impulse in some quarters to give praise to dissidents and those who were in opposition, while completely discrediting church institutions and officials, who are seen as having been "privileged" during the years of communist domination. But such a simple dichotomy can be unfair, as well as pastorally unhealthy, if this judgement is made without taking account of the actual nature of the "complicity", the measure of popular support for the political authorities and the realities of what was demanded for sheer survival in that repressive context. As the countries and peoples of Central and Eastern Europe enter into a new period after so many years of restrictions, their understanding of freedom is still a limited one; and a constructive policy for rebuilding these societies in the future cannot be determined solely on the basis of the immediate criticisms of some groups.

There is a strong tendency among the countries of Central and Eastern Europe to favour integration into a common Europe. The people want to resume their history, interrupted by the 1939-45 war, as full and free national ethnic entities. But after forty years of isolation, terror and despair, they also long for the joy of being one family. This process will face severe tests, of which the most difficult is the integration of minorities, migrants and refugees. On the other side, if the integration succeds, it brings with it the danger of uniformity, the temptation of reverting to European imperialism in which the unity of Europe makes the domination of the Third World all the more acute. The process will be a positive one only if it edifies Europe with a global vision while permitting the flowering of specific national values.

The countries in Eastern Europe should stop worrying pointlessly about the failure of the communist system. Discerning the times, they should engage in a process of infusing the continent with hope and humility. Europe could become an ecumenical arena in which the people, recognizing that the scale of global problems is too great for the resources we possess separately, actually do stop doing separately what they can do together. In the light of such a global vision, European countries should re-equip themselves for a new stage in history.

New theological issues. Several important theological issues have surfaced as a result of the political changes in Central and Eastern Europe and the questions they raise about the identity of societies which lived under the communist system. As we have said, the analysis of this period is very contradictory. Some churches might claim to have had an experience of resistance and opposition, even with a weak ecumenical dimension. In many cases, however, this resistance must be seen as confessional survival in a context dominated by the Roman Catholic Church (Poland, Hungary, to a certain extent Czechoslovakia). Other churches do not want to see these decades of oppression as a period of reference and therefore refer back to historical and cultural traditions that precede the communist era. But what all churches must do is to analyze the quality of their internal life and external action under these oppressive regimes.

In the search for a new political and cultural identity, religious values are being given renewed attention. Academic departments that based their philosophical systems and political strategies on atheism have suddenly been converted into centres for religious studies. There is a great interest in religious history and in Christianity as a part of it. Looking to the future, youth are very much concerned with the role of religious values. Sated with an empty and meaningless ideology, they now seek a system of values which does not impose boundaries to meaning. How open is our theology of religion to meeting and satisfying this hunger for the fundamental values of human life? How do the churches, invited to take part in the religious life of their nations, resist the siren song of the Constantinian symphony?

Indeed, the central concern in Europe today is the re-transmission of Christian values into the basis of European culture. The radical secularization which brutally separated the religious from daily life undermined not only religious belief but also the essence of European culture. [22] The disappearance of Christian culture has made Europe religiously illiterate. In the search for new cultural paradigms, however, many of those who put forward the model of European Christianity have taken for granted that European values are rooted in the *Latin* tradition. What is the *ecumenical* approach to religion and society in the context of a reunited European Christianity?

Ecumenical engagement has brought with it a sense of the undeniable urgency of Christian solidarity. This awareness calls us both to modify our Christian practice and theologically to reflect anew on political history. A new sense of confidence in what history may bring arises, not from a Marxist view of the development of the historical process, but from a theological understanding of the free intervention of the Holy Spirit, which makes a new Pentecost possible every day. This is to see history as an epiphany, a manifestation of the presence of the active and astonishing Spirit, who brings into existence, discerns, rejects and creates a new heaven and a new earth — whom God gives without measure at any time (John 3:34).

The recent historical experience of the Orthodox in Central and Eastern Europe can be extremely important for the ecumenical movement and the future of Christianity. Without going into detail about that experience, we should mention a few critical aspects:

All countries in economic crisis seek new social and political models. Burdened by the debts and deficits of previous periods, they are tempted to view the free-market economy of the so-called capitalist countries as a panacea. After forty years of communist experience, the churches must ask seriously, is this the way to build a new society?

Reconstruction of society has to be interpreted as a search for a new identity, both cultural and spiritual. Integral to this quest is the appropriation of past experience. Central and Eastern European Christians have learned, for example, the simple but extremely useful lesson that there is no liberty without liberation, no human rights without the struggle for political rights.

Acute problems surround the reorganization of the internal life and operations of the church. Many aspects of church life were restricted or forbidden during the communist era: public mission, lay movements, printing the Bible. Institutional limitations were especially trying for the Orthodox churches, which need a visible structure, a public space and time for their services. The relationship between the people and the church hierarchy is a delicate problem, demanding internal dialogue and conciliar life. The church's moral integrity is absolutely indispensable for the future of Orthodoxy.

There is also a need to integrate ecumenism into the internal discipline of the church, transforming it from a matter of ecclesiastical "foreign relations" into a part of the church's everyday life. This will not be easy, especially where the political situation has changed the balance between majority churches (in Hungary, Poland and Czechoslovakia, the Catholic churches considered themselves to be liberated by the recent events) and minority churches, on the basis of nationalistic influences. The revival of nationalism poses real dangers, especially where the minorities strongly supported the previous regime.

There will be tensions between the nationalistic policy of integration into a "common European house" and the confessional goal of being open to and united in conciliar fellowship with the whole *oikoumene*.

The new sitation in Central and Eastern Europe will release many energies, resources and possibilities for the benefit of the ecumenical movement. With political factors no longer restraining them, the Orthodox will bring new subjects into the ecumenical agenda, and infuse the movement with new people and new visions.

What consequences will all these changes have for the churches and the ecumenical movement? There is an irreversible evolution of common witness, mutual recognition and understanding of each other's positions.

At the same time, one can already discern new factors of division created by ethical issues, the rise of nationalism and the revival of uniatism.

In any analysis of the changes in the ecumenical scene in Europe we must remain modest, rigorously examining the positions defended and hypotheses advanced and viewing skeptically any claims to formulate a definite synthesis.

C. New local churches

The Orthodox diaspora — those communities and dioceses organized, definitely or provisionally, outside the territory of the traditional Orthodox countries — is a complex reality. Within the scope of this chapter we can touch on only some of the critical facets of it. Both in Western Europe and North and South America, it has developed in a haphazard manner in recent decades. No authority as had the force to organize this development in a systematic way. The canonical dimension of the diaspora question is part of a debate on the "autocephaly" and "autonomy" of the local church, which is one of the items for discussion in the preparatory meetings for the great Orthodox synod. Since there are dissenting groups within the diaspora, the diaspora itself became a canonical problem. What are the implications of the diaspora for inter-Orthodox unity, for the conciliar fellowship that Orthodoxy represents and for the growth of the ecumenical spirit in places where these communities are located?

The Orthodox in diaspora face three major problems:

1. *Canonical organization.* How do these dioceses maintain their link with the mother church or obtain autonomous status?[23] Many diaspora dioceses preserve direct contact with their churches of origin, with their bishops being appointed by the home synod. Others have organized themselves as independent dioceses of a "church in exile", against the mother church, with headquarters abroad. Still others have obtained a kind of autonomy and autocephaly which is not, however, recognized by all churches (the Ecumenical Patriarchate has received communities and dioceses of various origins under its jurisdiction but has not established new local churches).

2. *Pastoral integration* into their new cultural contexts. The diaspora communities seem naturally to identify themselves with one particular ethnic and cultural community. This has positive elements, but at the same time it severely limits their presence in the total mission work in a particular country. Even those communities who have claimed autonomous status face a permanent dilemma. On the one hand, they say that

their spiritual link with the original ethnic group is no longer essential; on the other hand, they cannot forget their historical roots and are not prepared to be immersed in the life of their new country. Russian Orthodox units in the West remain primarily Slavonic in their theological and cultural approach, and the seminary education of the new generation, which is called to work in the West, is still shaped by Eastern issues, as if the future priests did not have to meet Catholics and Protestants in their own lands.

3. *Ecumenical relations.* Orthodoxy as such has not benefited from the extraordinary privilege of a presence and mission in the midst of the Western world or the so-called Third World. The diaspora thus offers unique opportunities for intensive encounter and exchange of Christian experiences in which new ecclesiological ideas can be developed. Especially in the US and Canada, it also offers new possibilities for the Orthodox witness in the ecumenical community.

But rather than pursuing indigenization of the Orthodox faith in the West and becoming serious partners with other churches in the missionary and ecumenical life of a country or region, the Orthodox in diaspora have often been tempted to establish "organizations" to assist mother churches suffering from isolation and political pressure. They have forgotten that for mother churches it is more important to see the diaspora parishes and dioceses developed as full "local churches" in their situation, not remaining as an ethnic ghetto, but serving the construction of that particular nation, and being a model of local ecumenism in that given place.

Regrettably, there has been no inter-Orthodox exchange of experience between mother churches in the East and Orthodox communities in the so-called Western world. For ecumenical learning such dialogue is indispensable. As an illustration: while the Orthodox in most "traditionally Orthodox" countries encountered the Roman Catholic Church via uniatism and encountered Protestantism by way of sectarian and extremist communities practising proselytism, the Orthodox in diaspora have met these churches directly at home. The Orthodox mother churches could learn something from the experiences which their related churches abroad have had with Catholics and Protestants. To take another example: for several countries the missionary mind and ecumenical ethos of the Eastern Orthodox Church have been greatly determined by political pressures and social restrictions. By contrast, Orthodox communities in the diaspora today live in the so-called "free world"; but their ways and methods of doing mission in the new context are not yet consolidated, and therefore they offer no powerful point of reference for the mother churches.

The Orthodox diaspora must decide whether or not it is committed to a specific mission in its new environment and, accordingly, how to tackle the problems of communicating the Orthodox tradition and responding to ecumenical realities.

NOTES

[1] Cf. Francis House, "The Ecumenical Significance of the Patriarchate of Constantinople," *Ecumenical Review*, IX, 3 (April 1957), 310-20; Maximos of Sardes, *The Oecumenical Patriarchate in the Orthodox Church* (Thessaloniki: Patriarchal Institute for Patristic Studies, 1986).

[2] English translation in *Ecumenical Review*, XII, 1 (Oct. 1959), 79-82; Patelos, *The Orthodox Church in the Ecumenical Movement*, pp.40-43; and W.A. Visser 't Hooft, *The Genesis and Formation of the WCC* (Geneva: WCC, 1982), pp.94-97. For the text of the exchange of greetings between Castro and Dimitrios, see Appendix III.

[3] Cf. the chapter by Metropolitan (now Patriarch) Parthenios in Patelos, *op. cit.*, pp.242-47.

[4] Georges Khodr, "Le Christianisme antiochien," *Contacts*, XXX, 142 (1988), 121-28.

[5] For the history of the Jerusalem patriarchate see Maximos of Sardes, *op. cit.*, pp.284-87.

[6] Cf. Norman Horner, *Rediscovering Christianity Where it Began* (Heidelberg Press, 1974); and "Les Anciennes Eglises Orientales," *Unité Chrétienne*, no. 71 (July 1988).

[7] Cf. Iris Habib el Masri, *The Story of the Copts* (Middle East Council of Churches, 1978); and David F. Wright, "Councils and Creeds," in Tim Dowley, ed., *Handbook to the History of Christianity* (Grand Rapids: Eerdmans, 1977), pp.156-78.

[8] Cf. Mesrob Krikorian, "The Armenian Church and the WCC," *Ecumenical Review*, XL, 3-4 (1988), 411-16; and *Armenia: The Continuing Tragedy* (WCC CCIA Background Information, no. 1, 1984).

[9] Cf. Karekin Sarkissian, "The Armenian Church in Contemporary Times," in A. J. Arberry, ed., *Religion in the Middle East* (Cambridge: CUP, 1969); Aram Keshishian, *The Christian Witness at the Crossroads in the Middle East* (Beirut, 1981).

[10] An annotated bibliography on the Ethiopian Church, ed. by Jon Bonk, was published by Scarecrow Press (Metuchen, New Jersey, and London), 1984.

[11] Cf. Horner, *op. cit.*

[12] Cf. David Daniel, *The Orthodox Church of India* (New Delhi: Printaid, 1986); and Paulos Mar Gregorios, "A Reformation in the Malankar Orthodox Church," *Star of the East*, VIII, 1 (March 1986), 13-33.

[13] "Inter-Church Aid in the Middle East" is the subject of a chapter by Archbishop Athanasios (Coptic) in Kenneth Slack, ed., *Hope in the Desert* (Geneva: WCC, 1986), pp.71-77.

[14] "Aspects of Political Ethics in the Middle East" are discussed by Gabriel Habib in Koson Srisang, ed., *Perspectives on Political Ethics* (Geneva: WCC, 1983), pp.113-26.

[15] For some Orthodox perspectives on interfaith relations in the Middle East see Maurice Assad, "Faith and Culture in the Middle East," in John Mbiti, ed., *Confessing Christ in Different Cultures* (Geneva: WCC, 1977), p.132; Frieda Haddad, "Reflections on

Mission in the Arab Middle East," *International Review of Mission*, LXXVI, 301 (Jan. 1987), 72-77; Anastasios Yannoulatos, "Emerging Perspectives on the Relationships of Christians to People of Other Faiths," *ibid.*, LXXVIII, 307 (July 1988), 332-46.

[16] On the Russian Orthodox Church, see G. Razoumovsky, "Le mouvement oecuménique et l'Eglise russe," *Actes de la Conférence des Eglises Orthodoxes 1948* (Moscow Patriarchate, 1950), Vol. 2, p.200; "A Statement on Behalf of the Russian Orthodox Church," in T. Sabev, ed., *The Sofia Consultation: Orthodox Involvement in the WCC* (Geneva: WCC, 1982), pp. 78-88; Ioan Sviridov, "25 Years of the Russian Orthodox Church in the WCC," *Ecumenical Review*, XXXIX, 3 (July 1987), 346-51; and *WCC Member Churches in the Soviet Union* (Geneva: WCC, 1989). On the Romanian Orthodox Church, see Antonie Plamadeala, "The Orthodox Understanding of Ecumenism," in Sabev, *op. cit.*, pp.89-92; Nifon Mihaita, "The Romanian Orthodox Church and the Ecumenical Movement," *Ecumenical Review*, XXXIX, 3 (July 1987), 352-55; and *Romanian Orthodox Church* (Bucharest: Publishing House of the Romanian Patriarchate, 1987). On the Bulgarian Orthodox Church, see Sabev, *op. cit.*, pp.93-97.

[17] *Ecumenical Review*, XIV, 1 (Jan. 1962), 222.

[18] On the mission to the Slavs, see "The Witness of St Methodius: Orthodox Mission in the 9th Century" (reprinted from *International Review of Mission*, LXXIV, 249, April 1985).

[19] N. I. Mouraviev, "Le 500ème anniversaire de l'autocéphalie de la Sainte Eglise Orthodoxe Russe," in *Actes de la Conférence des Eglises Orthodoxes, 1948*, Vol. 1, p.51.

[20] Cf. the contribution by Eastern European members of the WCC Faith and Order Commission in *Sharing One Hope* (Geneva: WCC, 1979), pp.78-91.

[21] Cf. essays by Archbishop Kirill (Russian Orthodox), "Renewal of Humanity, Unity of the Church and the New Thinking," *Ecumenical Review*, XL, 2 (April 1988); and Paul Abrecht, "The Evolution of Ecumenical Social Thought, in P. Webb, ed., *Faith and Faithfulness* (Geneva: WCC, 1984), 114-19.

[22] Ion Bria, "Mission and Secularization," *International Review of Mission*, LXXVII, 305 (1988), 117-30.

[23] Cf. Nicholas Corneanu, "The Orthodox Diaspora," *Romanian Church News*, X, 2 (1980), 3-7; Maximos of Sardes, *op. cit.*, pp.309-43; Archbishop Paul of Finland, *Suggestions for Solutions to the Problem of the Orthodox Diaspora* (Valamo Monastery, 1979).

III. Orthodox Involvement in Ecumenism

The styles and forms of Orthodox participation in the WCC have evolved as the Council itself has developed.[1] At various points during the history of the WCC, different priorities and programmes have been predominant and different concepts or visions have served as the focal point of its activity. While recognizing that the churches must provide a pastoral response to the ever-shifting contexts in which they live and work, the Orthodox have always challenged this approach toward the search for unity.

Reciprocal research

At the beginning of their ecumenical involvement, the Orthodox felt obliged to unfold the doctrinal tradition they represented with historical objectivity and theological precision. This was done in order to clarify the differences and divisions which the churches had inherited from history. Serious generalizations — and oversimplifications — were expressed on all sides.

The Orthodox underlined that the theological and canonical legacy embodied in the Eastern tradition remains a reference point for the church universal. In this tradition the ecumenical movement could find inspiration and resources. They saw the reunion of West and East as a priority of the ecumenical movement, since the breaking of conciliar communion among the churches was historically the result of the schism of 1054 between Rome and Constantinople.

As a body which was not divided either by the schism of the eleventh century or the Reformation in the sixteenth, the Orthodox understood their vocation as guaranteeing the "ecumenism in time" which is at the heart of unity. To clarify and protect this position, they used to produce "separate" statements on questions of unity.

The Reformation churches underlined other principles and affirmations. There have always been ecclesiastical divisions and dogmatic divergences in church history; therefore, existing confessional differences must be tolerated as a legitimate fact of history. Nobody is responsible for the historical divisions, because we cannot translate the invisible divine unity into institutional terms. It was argued that there is no concern for doctrinal consensus in the New Testament; on the contrary, it gives evidence of a plurality of Christologies and ecclesiologies, some of them preserved in the modern confessional traditions. Moreover, there are areas of and opportunities for common Christian witness without firm doctrinal references.

During this early stage of ecumenism, the comparison of historical identities, theological methods and understandings of ecumenism was in the forefront. The text which best symbolizes this period is "The Church, the Churches and the World Council of Churches", often called the Toronto Statement (for the city where it was adopted by the WCC Central Committee in 1950).[2] At this stage the Orthodox detected in the Western approach a sort of dualism (vertical-horizontal, visible-invisible, institution-event) which would create a great deal of frustration.

Tension beyond unity

A second stage in ecumenical history is marked by a reinforced emphasis on common witness in a divided world. A sense of responsibility for historical divisions was translated into a growing interest in solidarity with people struggling for justice, peace and liberation. During this period the theology of liberation was forged out of the experience of base ecclesial communities and action groups and movements in the Third World. Before a world so divided, the centrality of the perspective of the unity of the church seemed to recede. Unity now had a new name and expression: solidarity of Christians with the people's struggles against the destruction of human life.

The period of transition from the stage of research and mutual rediscovery to taking concrete steps in the direction of a closer conciliar church fellowship was a critical one. Issues and tensions which were described in earlier times as normal and inevitable took an acute form verging on an "open crisis". In 1973 two large Orthodox churches raised serious questions about the contrasts between the horizontal and vertical dimensions of salvation and between doctrinal theology and contextual theologies. It was a moment of hesitation between clarifying the nature of divisions and discovering concrete forms of conciliar life:

> The task is demanding. The churches may find it so demanding that they hesitate to move forward. There is the acute danger that the search for unity

never gets beyond the state of search; that the churches remain standing on the threshold without entering the room they are called to live in together. But the demands must not be reduced.

The divided Christians must come so close to one another that they can recognize one another as belonging to one and the same communion. This means that WCC must work towards its own demise. There cannot be — and never has been — any question of regarding the fellowship as it now exists in the WCC as that one church whom we want to see restored. The goal is to be united in the one holy and apostolic church.[3]

It was paradoxically at the end of this period that the Central Committee of the WCC, with the participation of the Roman Catholic Church, adopted two important texts of ecumenical convergence: *Common Witness* (1981) and *Baptism, Eucharist, and Ministry* (1982).

As the churches recognized new frontiers and new challenges in their mission, efforts increased in spite of tensions and conflicts, to find a possible ecumenism for our times. Meanwhile, the Orthodox became increasingly oriented to direct bilateral dialogue, believing, as Kallistos Ware has said, "that more positive results are likely to be attained through these direct, bilateral conversations than through the assemblies and commissions of the WCC... In the years to come the Orthodox churches will probably concentrate their best upon these direct dialogues, and not upon the inter-Christian meetings organized from Geneva."[4]

Orthodox issues today

Commemoration of the WCC's fortieth anniversary in 1988 was an occasion to retrace the "ecumenical memory" of the years since Amsterdam.[5] Naturally, such preliminary descriptions gave only an incomplete image of the Council, but the general impression persists that the WCC still envisages unity primarily in terms of the churches' solidarity with people in their social and political needs. Reflections on the variety of theological approaches and forms of ecumenism also give the impression that some of the prevailing explicit statements and implicit assumptions about the nature of the church run counter to those of Orthodoxy.

Many Orthodox voices would say that the Council has not fulfilled its promises in the aspect of unity. But apart from the fact that Orthodox issues might seem to be marginalized by the contemporary ecumenical agenda, the Orthodox perceive a bias in favour of doctrinal positions which Orthodoxy does not allow.

To be sure, Orthodox issues have been a central concern of the WCC from the very beginning. Understandably, the Orthodox had an important role in formulating the Toronto Statement on the ecclesiological significance of the WCC, in changing the Basis of the WCC by introducing a clear affirmation of the Holy Trinity (1961) and in the long preparation and final adoption of the *Baptism, Eucharist and Ministry* text.

From time to time, as individual member churches or as a fellowship, the Orthodox have expressed critical responses to the WCC's basing of ecumenical priorities on the orientation of its social positions and political statements. The Third Preconciliar Conference (Chambésy, 1986) adopted a declaration on "Orthodoxy and the Ecumenical Movement", which seeks to articulate a clear Orthodox position on the "models of unity" proposed by the WCC.[6] The "desiderata" formulated by the Orthodox consultation in Sofia in 1981 were mainly of the same nature: changes in the structures of the WCC, increasing the number of Orthodox staff in Geneva, representation of all local churches in the Central Committee.

The Orthodox consider that the way in which subjects or themes are placed on the WCC agenda is often unhelpful. Since the beginning of the 1970s, the WCC methodology has favoured burning issues requiring immediate action. This has created the impression of exaggerating the experiences of action groups and movements, of ecumenism without specific concern for doctrine or for the "traditional" ecumenism followed by the historical churches. The WCC's success in relating urgent global issues to Christian historical and ethical perspectives has seemed to come at the expense of openness to the spiritual sensibilities of member churches, ignoring the fact that people work in various ways for the unity of the church.

This is what the Orthodox mean by saying that *Orthodox issues* have been bypassed or at least marginalized by the prevailing ecumenical understanding of the church and its unity. How can they find a structural entry point onto the current agenda of ecumenism? What is the WCC doing to break through this impasse?

But if some seem to fear the "vision" behind the Orthodox affirmation of permanent realities and values on which the ecumenical movement is built, there is also evidence today of a real desire to listen to the Orthodox and to learn from their tradition.

The Orthodox understand that they are real partners in the ecumenical debate by giving witness to vital concerns of considerable significance for the ecumenical fellowship at large. These questions are just as decisive for the Orthodox themselves; thus, any presentation of and reflection on these issues must be done in a spirit of self-criticism.

NOTES

[1] Cf. Emilio Castro, "The WCC and the Orthodox Church," in *Orthodoxie et Mouvement Oecuménique* (Chambésy: Centre Orthodox, 1986), pp.35-42.

[2] Reprinted often, including in *The First Six Years: 1948-1954* (Geneva: WCC, 1954). On the Orthodox and the "Toronto Statement" see Vitaly Borovoy, "The Ecclesiastical Significance of the WCC," *Ecumenical Review*, XLI, 3-4 (1988), 504-18; cf. *The Sofia Consultation*, p. 18: "Although it was recognized that the Toronto Declaration would need development or correction, its text was seen as an essential factor in the continuation of Orthodox membership in the WCC."

[3] M.M. Thomas and Philip Potter, "Response to the Declaration of the Ecumenical Patriarchate on the 25th Anniversary of the WCC," *Ecumenical Review*, XXV, 4 (Oct. 1984), 475.

[4] "Orthodoxy and the WCC," *Sobornost*, I, 1 (1979), 82.

[5] Cf. Georges Tsetsis, "The Meaning of the Orthodox Presence," *Ecumenical Review*, XL, 3-4 (1988), 440-72; Marlin VanElderen, "Varieties of Ecumenism," *One World*, no. 136 (June 1988), 11-16, and *Introducing the WCC* (Geneva: WCC, 1990).

[6] *Episkepsis*, no. 369 (Dec. 1986); cf. Nicholas Lossky, "Orthodoxy and Ecumenism," *One in Christ*, XVII, 2 (1981); John Romanides, "Presuppositions of Orthodox Ecumenism," in *The Sofia Consultation*, pp.65-68.

IV. The Essentials of the Tradition

At the heart of the history of the Eastern churches is the formation
of a concentric tradition around a few doctrinal issues. Indeed,
Orthodoxy has survived because it has always raised fundamental
issues of Christian faith which correspond to human religious needs,
moral attitudes and spiritual aspirations. Its authority depends on the
content of its revelation of God and on the accessibility, credibility
and reception of this revelation by the faithful. The Orthodox remain
confident about the central issues of humanity and its salvation — the
ontological exchange between God and humanity in the person of
Jesus Christ, the infinite mystery of God's revelation, the sacred
nature of the human person, the joy of the risen Christ — but they
recognize that the church, in transmitting this divine treasure, is under
the radical judgment of God. Jesus said that no one should reinforce an
old garment with a new piece of cloth, or put new wine into old
wineskins, because "new wine is put into fresh wineskins, and so both
are preserved" (Matthew 9:17).

What are the vital points around which Eastern thinking revolved,
which became the essentials transmitted as the holy Tradition?

First is the theology of the Trinity and, accordingly, the trinitarian
basis of the church and of spirituality. The Orthodox affirm the revelation
of God as the Triune God, as the unique *koinonia* of the Holy Trinity, in
which each person is recognized as a full person sharing the same
essence, power and glory. The theology of the Trinity contributes to a
deeper understanding not only of the human person, but also of the human
community.

The Orthodox made an important contribution to the ecumenical
convergence which affirms the trinitarian understanding of God as the
basis for ecclesial life. If today we dare to speak about the conciliar
process and eucharistic communion as something proper to the ecumenical community, it is precisely because we have reached a profound
consensus in our comprehension of the life of the Trinity:

Christians have only one point of reference to set standards for unity as well as justice — the life of the Holy Trinity as revealed in Jesus Christ and as experienced in the Eucharistic Community of the Spirit.

This life, however, cannot be reduced to a set of principles, rules or criteria. It is both a life that has to be lived and a vision that has to be seen in the Eucharistic Community.[1]

The icon of the Trinity, which became the symbol of the personal revelation of God, remains the icon of unity: "that they may be one, as we are one" (John 17:11). This transcendent communion in the Triune God is the norm of the communion among Christians, but it is also a discipline with real significance for the human community at large.

A second vital point of Eastern thinking is the eucharist as the sacrament of the transfiguration of matter. Inert matter, bread and wine, are really transformed by the power of the Holy Spirit into the living body and blood of Jesus Christ. The Tradition preferred to keep silent about the sacramental action behind the act of breaking the bread: it is a part of the mystery of how Jesus operates after his resurrection through the Holy Spirit.

Today the transfiguration of creation has become a serious issue for both Christian theology and secular science. How do we treat the creation in view of this organic link between matter and spirit, body and soul, death and life? All this is related to the affirmation of the resurrection of Christ as more than a general historical event. Christians are alive because they are joined to the risen Christ, and they die if they are separated from him by sin (cf. 2 Timothy 2:11). Each believer has to partake of his death and share in his passion. Every eucharist is a mediation of Christ's life into our life. He always lives to make intercession for us (Hebrews 7:25). The spirit of the Eastern Church is not based primarily on the membership of a visible community or on solitary personal discipleship, but on participation in the *koinonia* of the Holy Mysteries, by which one will be accepted among the number of those saints saved through Jesus Christ.

Since Pentecost, a new reality, an *ecclesia*, the Body of Christ, exists in the power of the Holy Spirit as an "icon", a sign and sacrament of the kingdom. The People of God is not merely a sociological community, but an historical projection of the apostolic group. The enduring presence in history of a visible Christian fellowship, which lives by overcoming all human barriers to peace, justice and unity, is part of the message of the gospel.

Orthodox ecclesiology is rooted in the reality of the *eucharistic liturgy*, and it therefore accentuates the priestly role of the lay faithful, "a chosen race, a royal priesthood, a consecrated nation, a people set apart" (1 Peter 2:9). Such an understanding of ecclesiology offers an essential input into conciliar life within the ecclesial body (relationship with hierarchy), into the edification of the fellowship *(koinonia)* of the church and into the presence and witness of Christians in the world. Life in Christ in history is a continuous people's liturgy, mystically representing the liturgy of heaven.

This also determines the understanding of mission as sanctification of nations. The Orthodox have also a particular understanding of *ethnos*. According to the traditional "symphony", the local church appears to identify itself with a particular national and cultural community. An *ethnos*, however, is not an unreached piece of the mosaic of humankind, but a potential local church with its own particularity. The Orthodox have, therefore, a maximalist understanding of both gospel and culture in every given place. The local church is a serious matter of people's identity.

This concentration on the *nation* has sometimes led to an overemphasis on independence, a mood of isolation, a narrow nationalism. The description of the local church must therefore integrate both the ecclesiological element and the national factor. At the turn of this century, the main ecclesiological problem was to establish local churches with autonomous and autocephalous status according to territorial and national principles. This was not only an organizational and jurisdictional preoccupation, but a serious matter of cultural and liturgical identity. But the autonomous and autocephalous local church is not a self-sufficient entity, with no need for the intercessions of and for the ecumenical fellowship or for the insights of Christians elsewhere.

The Eastern tradition gives enormous importance to the *catholicity* which is the work of the Holy Spirit. If misunderstood, this emphasis may lead to a "spiritualization" of Christian existence which emphasizes individual salvation or to justifying withdrawal into private ghettos that are intolerant of other styles of life. The Spirit may be misused to justify everything from domestic difficulties to ecclesiastical ambitions to intolerant theologies and pieties. What is required is to experience personal spirituality within the larger context of true fellowship.

We are tempted to identify the actions of the Spirit by following the mind of this world, forgetting what St Paul said: "Do not model yourselves on the behaviour of the world around you, but let your behaviour change, modelled by your new mind" (Romans 12:2). We have developed an understanding of the catholicity given by the Holy Spirit which is inadequate for the fellowship we seek in the ecumenical movement. We need constant regulation of expressions of ecumenical fellowship to prepare the way for realizing spiritual communion. The catholicity given by the Spirit is realized according to a dynamic which differs from the alliances and covenants we ourselves make — creating divisions, discriminations and barriers to protect our own interests. We need constantly to be reminded that the Holy Spirit we confess is not a created Spirit or an impersonal power of creation, but a personal God who recognizes the value and meaning of each person, each community, each nation, each people.

The Orthodox tradition has also dared to speak about the flow of *divine uncreated energies* into humanity and creation. Jesus does not merely bestow a share in his life; he gives *himself* in and through his Spirit. There is an element that derives directly from God. We are partakers of his own life. Not only does he impart whatever is good for us, not only does he release us and reconcile us to the Father, but he also gives us power to become children of God (John 1:12); he bestows all the fullness of his divinity (Colossians 2:9), all the riches of his very being. The new life originates in his life and arises from his cross and resurrection. It is he who provides life; he is himself what he provides. It is Christ himself who initiates us into this life. He himself is the content of the life we receive in his Spirit.

The meaning of Pentecost is seen in the light of this theology of exchange between our humanity and the Spirit of God. God sent the Holy Spirit not because he cannot act independently of us, not because he cannot save us alone, but because he has chosen to work through us and to save us as a community. God calls us to surrender ourselves to Christ in order that he may unite us to himself and work through us, thereby enhancing our freedom. The Holy Spirit came down upon the community not only to establish a covenant among us and to create a holy people of God (Isaiah 42:6), but also to introduce the personal reality of God into our own personal reality.

Because of its missionary and sacramental implications, pneumatology — the theology of the Holy Spirit — becomes the most immediately relevant section of theology. It imposes an attitude of humility on the church, which must leave room for the Spirit to blow wherever it wills.

One of the most important emphases in pneumatology is the *epiklesis* or invocation of the Spirit. The Holy Spirit is explicitly promised when the church offers the bread and wine for consecration. There is a point in the liturgy at which the prayers and offerings of the community through the priest come to an end. Remembering the cross and the resurrection of Christ, the priest then commends everything into the hands of God, the Son and the Spirit. Only the Spirit can change the substance of the elements and the lives of those who partake. The church can celebrate the eucharist only because it calls the Holy Spirit to do what it cannot do. The Spirit never fails to change our daily bread into the bread of eternity.

The Holy Spirit also grants the power to discern and witness to the truth in moments of despair and crisis. Christians are followers of Jesus' word that "if you continue in my word, you are truly my disciples, and you will know the truth, and the truth will make you free" (John 8:31-32). The Spirit not only discloses the revelation to each person but empowers us with the strength and wisdom to defend the truth of that revelation openly or in secret. Those who follow Jesus Christ all the way to the cross are under the protection of the Holy Spirit, the paraclete-counsellor of martyrs and confessors.

Theology is *doxology*. All theological formulations and arguments are offered to God as prayer and praise. This fundamental recognition can bring new insights into the hermeneutical debate and ecumenical theology. There should be no dichotomy between the ministry of theology and the ministry of worship, because both are part of the communication of the mystery of faith. To be sure, academic theology is not always a suitable instrument for mediating the faith. In celebrating the faith, people go behind the creeds, doctrines and dogmas. The church therefore cannot conceive of theology outside the liturgical community or without the spiritual experiences of prayer and contemplation. The living teaching must be spelled out in a living doxology.

Theology is a deep and permanent existential knowledge which transcends verbal and conceptual expressions. The Orthodox have used hymnography and iconography constantly to challenge the language and images applied to God. The symbolic language of theology evokes adoration and prayer. It takes place in an act of personal invocation and communion with God; prayer, says D. Staniloae, is the gateway to theology.

Theology embraces a diversity of areas of church life: liturgy, music, hymns, icons, literature, symbols, architecture, art. It prefers organic language to conceptual, propositional terminology. In spite of the Western scholastic influence on Orthodox theology, especially at the end of the nineteenth and the beginning of the twentieth century, this fundamental character has remained: a doxological and spiritual approach to expressing the faith, which is preserved in the experiences of saints rather than in decisions by a magisterium.

NOTE

[1] Ion Bria and C. Patelos, eds., *Orthodox Contributions to Nairobi*. (Geneva: WCC, 1975), p.28.

V. Ecclesiological Emphases

The "catholicity" of local churches

At the heart of Eastern ecclesiology lies the faith of the Orthodox Church in the oneness of the church, the *Una Sancta*.

> There can be no churches (in the plural) except as manifestations of the one true church. The unity of the church does not mean creating a worldwide organization, often called structural unity. The one church cannot be created by putting all the local churches and individual denominations into one worldwide structure... It is this church that manifests itself in its catholic fullness in each local church; the local church is not to be conceived of as part of some other reality called the universal church, which is sometimes understood as composed of local churches.[1]

The church is the visible reality of the people of God, assembled at Pentecost in the power of the Holy Spirit, which bears witness to God's revelation, to the presence and action of Jesus Christ in history. In and through this church, God calls and unites all nations to become his own pilgrim people and to live as a "sacrament" of his kingdom which has come and is coming.

Intrinsically, the debate about the "universal" and the "local" is one about the nature of the church, not about the organizational structure of different levels of Christian community. The *ecclesia* of Pentecost has its supreme image in the *koinonia* of the Holy Trinity. Here is a unique communion in which person is person and community is community. As the trinitarian persons share the same nature they recognize each other as full persons. The icon of the Trinity remains the icon of the church, of its unity and communion: "Christians have only one point of reference to set standards for unity as well as justice — the life of the Holy Trinity as revealed in Jesus Christ and as experienced in the eucharistic community of the Spirit. This life, however, cannot be reduced to a set of principles, rules or criteria. It is both a life that has to be lived and a vision that has to be seen in the eucharistic community".[2]

The "catholic" church is not just a remote reality which we confess in the creed. It is also experienced in each local church as the eucharistic community presided over by the bishop with his presbyters and deacons. A great deal of confusion is caused when these words "universal" and "local" are used without their eucharistic understanding and limited to a geographical and organizational interpretation. The Orthodox have tried to develop this eucharistic sense of universality:

> In the course of history circumstances often necessitated the creation of larger ecclesial units, such as the metropolis, the patriarchate, the autocephalous church, etc. However, in the function of these units, national, social or cultural and racial divisions should not distort the original eucharistic understanding of the church. The canonical structure of the Orthodox Church, as it was formed in the early centuries, has helped and can still help to protect Orthodoxy from succumbing to such dangers. [3]

Precisely because the local church is a sign of the extension of the kingdom of God on earth, "universal" and "local" are not to be understood as two separate ecclesiological realities. The universal church is not a federation of independent churches united hierarchically for institutional or administrative purposes. It represents a communion of local autocephalous churches which have inner eucharistic and canonical unity. [4] Within this communion, every local church holds a "catholic" view, because the presence of the one Holy Spirit is given to the church as a whole as a guarantee of its unity and truth. At the same time, the local church has the freedom, under its bishop and self-governing synod, to express its own identity and concrete vocation, taking into account the pastoral needs of its people in their place.

Each local celebration of the eucharist is thus complete and universal. At one and the same time it involves a concrete community (the local church), the whole church and the entire creation. Each local church is recognizable through the one who presides at the liturgy and who unites it with the universal church:

> This catholic nature of the church which is revealed in the eucharist is safeguarded through the office of the bishop. The specific ministry of the bishop is to transcend in his person all the divisions that may exist within a particular area, and also to relate a local church to the rest of the local churches both in space and in time. This link is sacramentally expressed in the synodal consecration of bishops. Because of the character of episcopacy it is essential that there should exist only one bishop in a given area and that all eucharistic communities should acquire their ecclesial authenticity through his ministry.

> The local church, therefore, is not necessarily present in every eucharistic assembly but in the episcopal diocese through which each eucharistic gathering acquires its catholic nature.[5]

The unity of the local and universal church has its ultimate source in the confession of the same apostolic faith (holy Tradition) and its ultimate expression in sharing the same eucharist. On the one hand, the Eastern tradition has stated clearly that the broken unity in faith is not a simple matter of theological diversity but something that touches the common confession of faith. On the other hand, the common reception of the apostolic faith is fundamental in relation to the sacramental and eucharistic communion. Full eucharistic communion will not be possible until unity of faith is achieved.

What is the exact theological content of the unity of the church? It is a God-established mark of the Body of Christ: "So all of us, in union with Christ, form one body, and all parts of it belong to each other" (Romans 12:5). The promises and assurances in the discourse and prayer of Christ (John 13:31-17:26) were fulfilled at Pentecost, when Christ came in the Spirit and formed those who believed in him into his body, the church:

> Thus Pentecost is the birthday of the church, and the continuing experience in history of those who have since joined the communion of those illumined and glorified in Christ. It is thus that the prayer of Christ for unity (John 17:11) was fulfilled and is being fulfilled.
>
> It is also a unity which is to be consummated and manifested when Christ appears in glory; devoid of all spots and blemishes, freed from sin, perfectly united to the head of the body, Christ, sharing in the life of the triune God, "that they all may be one, even as we are one" (John 17:11). This unity in the triune God, with Christ in us and we in Christ, Christ in the Father and the Father in Christ by the Spirit, as an eschatological reality, is the standard and norm for the unity of the church today. This church which is the "fullness of Christ" cannot itself be judged by us, for Christ with his church is the Judge of the world itself.[6]

The Eastern tradition sees catholicity as expressing the church's obedience to the apostolic calling to share "all the truth" (John 16:13) with all nations in their specific historical and cultural situations. Catholicity is not a quest for global expansion, organizational uniformity or jurisdictional centralization. It is based on an understanding of the church as open to the *oikoumene*, an understanding of the "catholic" character of the local community as a eucharistic fellowship gathered around its bishop.[7] It is also grounded on the understanding of mission as a sanctification of all "nations" with their own specific identity, culture and ethos. These views have implications for the organization of the local churches. The very existence of local churches is evidence of this Orthodox catholicity, which implies the manifestation and realization of what belongs to the whole people of God in concrete local situations, in each instance and place, at all times and in all places.

This concentration on internal, qualitative catholicity has sometimes led to a sense of independence and isolation, a narrow nationalism. But the local church is a living reality in continuous reconstruction and renewal not only because of distinctive factors in its own national context but also because of the efforts it makes as a result of ecumenical involvement. When the local church enters into the ecumenical circuit, the quality of its solidarity changes.

Therefore, the local church, having its own catholic character, should be a point of departure for a movement which takes it beyond its canonical limits.

> Whatever motives may have determined the birth of this or that auto-cephalous church, the unity of the Orthodox world should not be thought of as that of a federation of juxtaposed and self-sufficient sovereign churches but rather as a unity in diversity. Alert to the voice of the Spirit, they will be able to avoid rivalry and the spirit of domination by acknowledging their equal dignity in Christ. This *convivialité* will permit each of them, within the limits of the territory historically assigned to it, to put down its roots in the culture of its people and to help the full development of that people in justice and freedom. [8]

The Holy Spirit and the church

Recent Orthodox ecclesiology underlines the importance of understanding the church and its unity in the broad perspective of the *oikonomia* of the Holy Spirit:

> The coming of the Holy Spirit in the church is not an isolated historical event but a permanent gift which gives life to the church, ensuring its existence in the history of humanity, making possible its witness to the inaugurated kingdom of God. The Holy Spirit is the divine power whereby the church is able to obey the command of the Risen Lord: "Go forth then and make all nations my disciples" (Mt. 28:19); "Go forth to every part of the world and proclaim the Good News to the whole creation" (Mk. 16:15; cf. Lk. 24:47 and Acts 1:8). This permanent Pentecostal outpouring of the Spirit on the church is a reality in the church's worship, public prayer and the Sunday celebration of the Eucharist, but it overflows the limits of ecclesial worship and constitutes the inner dynamic which gives character to all expressions of, and all activities in, the life of the church. [9]

Pentecost continues to enable the people of God to hold the Tradition in ways the Spirit wills. The Eastern Church understands this continuity as ensured by an episcopal ministry consecrated in the apostolic succession. But the church is built on the foundation of the apostles and prophets, with Christ Jesus himself as its main cornerstone (Ephesians 2:20). This view of the church does not prevent the participation of all in the building up of the body. The wholeness — koinonia — of the body implies that all categories of the people of God share fully in "all the truth". This is the charismatic ministry of the people of God, who are transformed by the power of the Holy Spirit into the "living stones" of the church.

Hence the Orthodox insistence on the cultivation of a theology of the Holy Spirit in the ecumenical movement. The Spirit comes from above and runs ahead of our history and projects. The Spirit can do what human and natural forces are not capable of doing. The eucharistic liturgy makes clear that a moment comes when human effort and action end in order to be assumed, transformed and judged by the Spirit. Fundamentally, the building of ecumenism is not an enterprise based on human and material forces. The church must contribute an immense effort, but before and through the church the Holy Spirit is working to construct an ecumenical community. Why then does the Holy Spirit not lead us into open communion with others? Perhaps because we are too concerned with what we put into the liturgy and not concerned enough with what the Spirit does, and with the eucharist as a wonderful uniting element.

Western theology has not spoken very explicitly and concretely about the Holy Spirit as a person and action of the triune God. Spirit language and thinking, brought forcefully into ecumenical discussion by the Orthodox, has thus represented a corrective influence which has enabled theology to become more trinitarian, thereby opening new understandings of the nature of the church and its unity. It makes a great difference for the ecumenical community to say that the Holy Trinity is the image of the church, the model of the human community.

A theology of the Spirit can also help us to recover the distinctive meaning of Christian spirituality, underlining the too often ignored biblical values in which Christian identity is rooted. It is a reminder of the apostolic vocabulary related to the Spirit: love, joy, peace, patience, kindness, generosity, faithfulness, gentleness, self-discipline (Galatians 5:24). It encourages people to deepen their spiritual roots, to find a new style of life and new forms of Christian community and solidarity. Of course, not all human experiences and endowments can be classified under Christian spirituality without discernment.

When Spirit language is applied to the church, ecclesiological terminology moves from the "People of God", which appears to be a rather institutional definition in the prophetic perspective, to the more inclusive "Body of Christ", which implies a eucharistic-sacramental understanding of the "fellowship — *koinonia* — of the Holy Spirit".

The WCC's 1983 Vancouver assembly placed strong emphasis on the trinitarian context of the Christian theology of the church. The assembly began with a meditation on the icon of the Holy Trinity, an enduring symbol of the ecumenical movement. Subsequent development of appreciation for the trinitarian aspect of theology was reflected in the pneumatological theme of the Canberra assembly in 1991: "Come, Holy Spirit, Renew the Whole Creation". The prayer "Come, Holy Spirit" is a recognition of the pneumatological entry point into all the realities facing the churches today. We have to see, for example, the unity of the people of God in the framework of the unity of the human community. Can the church exist without involving all people? Other issues can also be understood from the perspective of the Holy Spirit: creation, social order, culture, education, solidarity, political liberation. There is no advance in the search for unity without openness to and cooperation with the Holy Spirit, who reveals the elements and events that transform both personal and community life.

Unity of the church — a eucharistic vision

The life and witness flowing from the eucharistic act itself demand close attention. Recent references in ecumenical theology to a *eucharistic vision* reflect a unique Eastern contribution to contemporary ecumenical thinking. Two chapters (20 and 26) of the Eucharist section of the *Lima Document*, make evident the influence of Orthodox theology on such a broad eucharistic perspective. They merit quoting in full:

> 20. The eucharist embraces all aspects of life. It is a representative act of thanksgiving and offering on behalf of the whole world. The eucharistic celebration demands reconciliation and sharing among all those regarded as brothers and sisters in the one family of God and is a constant challenge in the search for appropriate relationships in social, economic and political life (Matt. 5:23f; 1 Cor. 10:16f; 1 Cor. 11:20-22; Gal. 3:28). All kinds of injustice, racism, separation and lack of freedom are radically challenged when we share in the body and blood of Christ. Through the eucharist the all-renewing grace of God penetrates and restores human personality and dignity.

The eucharist involves the believer in the central event of the world's history. As participants in the eucharist, therefore, we prove inconsistent if we are not actively participating in this ongoing restoration of the world's situation and the human condition. The eucharist shows us that our behaviour is inconsistent in face of the reconciling presence of God in human history: we are placed under continual judgement by the persistence of unjust relationships of all kinds in our society, the manifold divisions on account of human pride, material interest and power politics and, above all, the obstinacy of unjustifiable confessional oppositions within the body of Christ....

26. As it is entirely the gift of God, the eucharist brings into the present age a new reality which transforms Christians into the image of Christ and therefore makes them his effective witnesses. The eucharist is precious food for missionaries, bread and wine for pilgrims on their apostolic journey. The eucharistic community is nourished and strengthened for confessing by word and action the Lord Jesus Christ who gave his life for the salvation of the world. As it becomes one people, sharing the meal of the one Lord, the eucharistic assembly must be concerned for gathering also those who are at present beyond its visible limits, because Christ invited to his feast all for whom he died. Insofar as Christians cannot unite in full fellowship around the same table to eat the same loaf and drink from the same cup, their missionary witness is weakened at both the individual and the corporate levels.

These specific emphases from the Eastern tradition prevent the reduction of the debate on ecclesiology to sociological and ideological considerations. Ecumenism, which is sometimes criticized for having become a theology of solidarity with the people, must be grounded in a eucharistic vision which is concerned both with the fellowship of the Holy Spirit and with oikoumene.

Rewriting Orthodox ecclesiology

In the 1930s there was a great deal of attention to the need to purify Orthodoxy of "foreign influences" and to recapture the Hellenism of the church fathers by a "neo-patristic synthesis" (First Congress of Theological Faculties, Athens, 1936). It was argued that the identity of the Orthodox tradition was being obscured by systematic theology from Latin scholastic sources (mainly through the Greek and Russian schools of theology). Serious interpretation was required to extirpate these influences, which created a false image of Orthodoxy.

By mid-century, as we saw earlier, Orthodoxy was often being presented as "mystical theology", whose nature could be disclosed to Western cultures only by invoking the mystery of the church. Interpretation and communication were therefore limited.

During the last few decades there has been an abundance of material on spirituality, mainly from the isichast tradition, sometimes presented in a rather dry form, sometimes with serious theological analysis. The intention is to renew the idea of sanctification as a way of being holy in the world; but the implications of ascetic discipline for social ethics, especially in a materialistic society, have not been treated fully.

More recently, a rich literature has been devoted to the visible structure and sacramental unity of the church, especially to the reality and symbolism of the episcopate. In line with a view of the church as a mystery, many theologians have spoken of the mystical, typological position of the bishop. The episcopate is a visible structure exercising a power that gives certainty to the life and mission of the church. It is a structure which gives the church a status of certainty, but such a church cannot take risks in its affirmations and acts.

Church/symbol — church/community

The key issues facing Eastern Christianity today are linked with the tension between a defensive and magisterial way of presenting the church as a symbolic, mystical reality, and the history, life and mission of the concrete communities that form the visible church.

We cannot idealize the church by ignoring the people who carry the burden of tradition in different situations. We must reflect on what people are actually doing to identify what is emerging in contemporary Christianity. What are the most significant subjects for the life and mission of the churches? What experiences and practices among Orthodox today need to be recognized and examined?

Transmission of the Tradition in the post-Constantinian period

Orthodox often claim a special responsibility to witness to the Christian faith as it was transmitted throughout the centuries. But the way they interpret the Tradition often gives little attention to the distinction between the content of faith and the process of its transmission.

All tradition is both received and transmitted. These two aspects are inseparable. Tradition is an invitation to transmit the faith and thus a movement of *mission*.

The history of the Orthodox Church demonstrates how cultural context, missionary environment, forms of establishment and other factors influence the reception or rejection of Christian tradition. Transmission of the tradition is thus a complex development, not a simple process.

For example, on many issues the church in the Constantinian period adopted a more conservative position than the early apostolic church had taken. Some instances are the attitude towards violence, limitations on a great variety of ministries in the church, uniformity of schools of theology, restrictions against women, clerical understanding of the liturgy. Theologically, the Constantinian church did not take the same Christocentric approach to social issues as the apostolic church. Christology became a matter of intellectual and philosophical dispute rather than an inspiration for building a new society. In sacralizing the famous "symphony" between emperor and patriarch, the church left concern for Christian society in the hands of the state. The "sociality" of the church appeared to be more important than a prophetic role in society. Captivated by the programme of the empire, the church seldom expressed a very critical attitude towards what the state was doing.

These major shifts in the practices and emphases of the church might have created an open crisis. But that did not happen, because this period coincided with the golden age of the fathers of the church. The great patristic tradition must be understood primarily as a counter-movement, correcting the extremes of the fourth-century Constantinian "symphony" in a way that avoided a radical crisis between the apostolic church and the Constantinian church.

An element of the Constantinian "symphony" was the establishment of a conciliar system — the council of bishops — to decide on a common doctrine of faith on which the unity of the Christian empire could be built. A particular understanding of the apostolic succession of the bishops appeared which conceded to them the right to make pronouncements of faith. Their doctrinal authority was based on their consecration in the apostolic succession, leaving little room for consideration of their spiritual capacity to discern the truth on the basis of the experience of Pentecost. In some periods of church history, this led to crisis situations in which ecclesiastical authorities did not speak the word of God clearly or defend gospel values. It is the vocation of church historians to illuminate these conflicts between those who claimed authority purely on the basis of their episcopal consecration and those who became church leaders because of their spiritual experience.

The *typology* of the church, as introduced in recent ecclesiological discourse, has sometimes left the impression that the church may live as a symbolic entity and that its personal, historical and sociological reality is irrelevant. The visible structure is seen as a symbolic representation disconnected from the life and salvation of the people of God. But how can the church-as-symbol exist without the church-as-community? Symbolism and reality must coincide, and the history and praxis of Christians must be taken seriously.

The danger of incoherence between church-as-symbol and church-as-community is a real one, demanding a new debate on how the church is to be understood pastorally, a kind of *ecclesiology in flesh and bones*. At the beginning of the 1960s, many were talking about a *new Reformation*; a decade later, after the Second Vatican Council, ecclesiological categories such as *New Church* and *New Christianity* were being used. But all these remained abstractions without an effort to give reality to them.

One aspect of this debate is how the community functions as the "carrier" or "subject" of the church. In many places there is a renewed concern for the people as carriers of the tradition and a new approach to the continuity of the church. Tradition and succession have to do with passing on the experience of the people who rightly claim to have the assistance of the Spirit. No one external has control over the apostolic character of the church; in fact, there is no theological support for considering the ecclesiastical authority as appointed by God to master all truth. The people of God have their own quality and right to voice the gospel, beyond any magisterial manipulation.

This means that we must give a reality to our ecclesiology of the local church, the temple of the Holy Spirit in flesh and bones. We can no longer ignore the ecclesiology of "parishioners", the faithful members of the community who are the real "co-workers" with God in maintaining the faith on earth.

The great tradition of *conciliarity* must be renewed. We are so overwhelmed by an interpretation of the history of salvation and of the church as an unending series of conflicts, polarities, tensions and religious wars that we have forgotten the healing dimension of salvation and the story of conciliar practice among different groups.

The recent emphasis on "conciliar fellowship" represents an indisputable theological development. But here, too, we must go beyond abstractions. Certain theological areas need special attention. For example, all churches are facing difficulties in transmitting traditional doctrine as such. Christians feel increasingly free to confess or to disregard the fundamentals of faith as they were proposed in the past. This points up the urgency of formulating an explanation of faith with contemporary relevance in order both to face these internal difficulties and to surmount ancient doctrinal divergences.

We must also keep alive the conciliar process around *peace* and *justice* as a common ground of the ecumenical community. The false dichotomy between an "ecclesial" approach to unity and a "social" approach must be abandoned once and for all. Visible ecclesial unity around major human concerns and values should remain one of the orientations of the ecumenical endeavour, for conciliar fellowship implies not only attention to confessional positions and tradition, but also a change in the discipline of the church in its relations with people and society.

We have seen that the churches have given priority to certain issues at various stages of ecumenical history: for many decades, ecclesiology was the point of concentration; in recent decades it has been Christian involvement in building up a community in solidarity with the poor, oppressed and marginalized. The future of humanity and creation, salvation of human beings and values, in both their personal and social dimensions, are serious concerns of today. We should be free and open to enter into a conciliar process in order to arrive at common convictions and commitments.

Church-icon and people of faith

Recent developments have demonstrated how Orthodox churches have maintained vigorous roots in the life of the people of their respective countries. Again, we can only single out a few examples.

The 1988 celebration of the millennium of the baptism of the Russian people activated the faith of multitudes in the Russian church. The experience of the Russian church, considered by many as reduced by persecution almost to non-existence, has revealed that the people do not abandon their faith even in times of crisis.

In that same year, the celebration of 900 years since the founding of the monastery of Patmos became a real demonstration of the Greek people around their church leaders. An Easter liturgy, a procession with the relics of a saint or the feast of a saint may naturally become a popular festival in which faith and culture, *ecclesia* and *ethnos* are intermingled. The Greek Orthodox Church has extraordinary potential for mission, education and service, because it includes the largest number of educated lay persons.

In Damascus, Patriarch Ignatios courageously confronts challenges threatening the life of the faithful in Syria and Lebanon, where people sing the liturgy while shellfire shakes the church building. His compassion with the people has made him one of the most influential voices in the Middle East as well as in the Orthodox communities around the world.

A powerful example is the Armenian church and people, with their capacity to endure suffering and martyrdom again and again in their common history. The Armenian church today is a central force in the people's struggle for national integrity.

In Egypt, the spirituality of the cross and the austerity of the Coptic church have helped the people to be resilient as a nation and culture throughout their long history. The popular character of the church has been renewed by Pope Shenouda, one of the great catechists of our time.

These and many other experiences have something to say, not only to Marxist sociologists and historians, but also to theologians who have speculated about the "post-Constantinian" context, "secularization", the "minority situation", the *Volkskirche* or the "institutional church". Of course, one must assess these situations with care and realism, but it is clear that church-symbol and people of faith is a reality of our time.

Having churches with such a deep sense of commitment to their people among its members has significant consequences for the policy, programmes and structures of the WCC. Quite rightly, the defence of minorities is an item high on the WCC agenda. But what is the WCC's responsibility in the case of *majority* churches? How does it benefit from the potential and resources of the people of these churches?

These churches should in turn be asked the following: What is the specific ministry of a church in a majority situation to the communities who represent minorities in their country? What is the meaning of "establishment" today, which enables a church to preserve its autonomy in the midst of powerful nations and systems?

Methodology, theological language and rhetoric of unity

We conclude this chapter with some observations about another factor which may lie at the root of separations: differences in theological method and orientation. The basic framework in which many ecumenical issues are discussed is still unfamiliar to the Eastern churches. A certain methodology is taken for granted in ecumenical studies which tends from the beginning to marginalize the Orthodox. This is why many major trends in ecumenical thought have been neither confirmed nor challenged by the Orthodox. But the diversity of methodologies should not just be ignored. The Orthodox should not be forced to accept any particular interpretation as normative and should be allowed to propose their own methodology.

After years of intensive analysis of historical material (sometimes with the help of ideology), there is a growing interest in contemplation and spiritual experience as a theological method. Through prayer, liturgy and worship, theology is trying to rediscover the link between analytical interpretation and spiritual contemplation. Great interest is being shown in artistic and poetic expressions of spiritual experiences generated by human history, including political struggle.

What is new is the importance given to spirituality (life in the Spirit) for understanding the reality of God, creation and history. Young people are invading places of pilgrimage, holy places, where they can find a living and tangible expression of the experience of God. There is a hunger for God. Western Christianity of the Reformation feared mystics, religious orders, iconography and saints, regarding them as nebulous at best, distracting and harmful at worst. The lives of the saints were seen as literature for simple folk, not as anything with theological relevance.

The WCC's current emphasis on relating theology and spiritual formation is timely and important. Morover, not only theology but also mission and witness are based on spirituality — the discipline of following Jesus, receiving the holiness of God. One can foresee development of the theme of spirituality as a common ground in our ecumenical pilgrimage, doing away with negative comparisons of the Western and Eastern spiritualities or Eastern and African spiritualities. A new tool is, therefore, available for theological reflection and work.

More and more, the criticism is heard that the theological basis of certain ecumenical actions and statements is inappropriate or not explicit enough. The impression is that the ecumenical movement does not know how to relate questions of faith and social questions, because it is blocked at the crossroads between theology and politics. Hence, there is a crisis of ecumenical action, because the Christocentric approach to social questions is not an active criterion.

Are we encouraging the binding of Christians to a social ethics or a system of values which does not lead to the focal point: the person of Jesus Christ? Are we hesitating on the preliminary theology of our experience? Is not the choice of faith already made when we treat social questions?

The criterion for whether one's option and involvement are true or false is not the credibility of the action but the Christocentric basis of the commitment. The source of our involvement is the new reality we received in the incarnation and resurrection of Jesus Christ. We are involved with the poor and the oppressed because he gave his life for them. Our involvement is true or false inasmuch as it refers back to the new reality already given in Jesus Christ. The old tradition of a Christ-ocentric approach to social issues ("you did it to me"; cf. Matt. 25:40) needs to be renewed.

Within the WCC one can find great variety not only in theological insights, missionary perspectives and ecclesiological positions, but also in the vocabularies of unity. These are not always coherent. The terms "unity" and "ecumenism" are used in different contexts with different meanings, creating misunderstanding and confusion. There are also some key definitions in ecumenical language. For example, for the Orthodox, "tradition" embodies the struggle to transmit the faith from generation to generation, from place to place. "Tradition" means faithfulness and transmission, and is a key to understanding both mission and unity. Because several aspects of the Orthodox rhetoric of unity are easily misunderstood, we need more clarity on this subject.

NOTES

[1] Bria, ed., *Jesus Christ — the Life of the World*, pp.12-13.

[2] *Orthodox Contributions to Nairobi*, p.28.

[3] Tsetsis, ed., *Orthodox Thought*, p.24.

[4] Cf. D. Popescu, "The Local Church and Conciliar Fellowship," *Ecumenical Review*, XXIX, 3 (1977), 265-72; Ion Bria, "Ecclésiologie," *Unité Chrétienne*, no. 70 (May 1983), 46-88.

[5] Tsetsis, ed., *loc. cit.*

[6] *Jesus Christ — the Life of the World*, p.13.

[7] John Zizioulas, "The Local Church in a Eucharistic Perspective," in *In Each Place* (Geneva: WCC, 1977), pp. 50-61; cf. Stanley Harakas, "The Local Church: an Eastern Orthodox Perspective," *Ecumenical Review*, XXIX, 2 (Apr. 1977), 141-53.

[8] *Orthodox Contributions to Nairobi*, p.31. Nissiotis remarks that "a non-Orthodox can enter into the life and mind of the Orthodox churches only if he is ready to appreciate the popular religiosity of their members and the simplicity of their appreciation of national and church history, as well as their uncritical acceptance of the sacramental life that sanctifies their entire social, family and professional life" (*Orthodox Theological Education*, p.47).

[9] Tsetsis, ed., *op. cit.*, pp. 38f.; cf. Damaskinos Papandreu, "Einheit der Kirche aus orthodoxer Sicht," *Oekumenische Rundschau*, XX (1971), 262-82; John Meyendorff, *Catholicity and the Church* (Crestwood NY: St Vladimir's Press, 1983).

VI. Orthodox Challenges to the Ecumenical Movement

Theology of the Holy Trinity

This is perhaps the most substantial insight the Orthodox Church has brought into ecumenical theology in the period since the WCC's Vancouver assembly (1983). This has been done in terms of relating diverse aspects of ecclesial life — liturgy, mission, diaconia and unity — as arising out of a profound experience of the Holy Trinity. The *koinonia* of the Holy Trinity, the one God, fashions every reality.

The theology of the Trinity is linked with a debate on the nature of the church. The Orthodox churches are not satisfied to reduce the question of unity to the organizational structure of different levels and sectors of contemporary Christendom. For them, part of the ecumenical theological convergence is affirming that the trinitarian understanding of God is the basis for eccesial life.

The Orthodox believe that the ecumenical movement should faithfully embody that understanding of the nature of God, and what God offers to the world in his Son and communicates to the world in his Spirit. The edification and persistence in history of a living and visible Christian fellowship, overcoming all barriers, is possible only if it is really created and granted by God as the extension of his communion.

"Undivided church"

The Orthodox insist that the ecumenical movement cannot exist without understanding the relevance of the "undivided church" for the contemporary response to historical divisions among churches and Christians. *"Undivided church, divided Christians"* — this is the primary reality which confronts the ecumenical movement.

The ecumenical idea emerged out of the need to re-unite Christians who have been divided for centuries and to heal their fragmentation. Non-communication and even excommunication separated Eastern and Western Christianity for nearly a thousand years. Already after the council of Chalcedon (451) the Oriental churches separated themselves from Byzantine Christendom. Between the 9th and 11th centuries, universal Christianity split into two main parts, each with its own jurisdiction and culture. The 16th-century Reformation created another split within European Christendom. The ensuing confessional divergences and cultural conflicts created a complex situation marked by polemics which made conciliar order and mutual recognition impossible. This tendency to schism and confessional division should be examined objectively.

In becoming participants in the ecumenical movement, the Orthodox have understood their task as giving a particular witness to the ancient traditions of the church from apostolic times when the church was undivided. Through this concept, they read the history of Christianity. Their vocation is to express this reality and to relate it to different parts of the ecumenical community. What is the real sense of this ancient "undivided church"? According to Prof. J. Karmiris, unity means return to the existing "pentarchy" of the five patriarchates of the ancient church (Rome, Constantinople, Alexandria, Antioch, Jerusalem).

The idea of conciliarity belongs to the very nature of the "undivided church":

> The Orthodox believe that a council presupposes and expresses the unity and the catholicity of the church. A council can only be held if all its members fully recognize each other as belonging to the same church of Christ, guided by the same spirit. A council is an assembly representing local churches, each possessing, in unity with the others, the fullness of catholicity, witnessing together to the same truth, aiming at maintaining unity which is perhaps threatened and possibly also admitting that some do not belong to the koinonia of the church. [1]

The "undivided church" is sometimes affirmed in a way that suggests that it is a peculiar model which never existed in history. But the position is stated clearly: unity means the overcoming of the divisions which have arisen among historical confessions and the realization of communion in the unique church of Christ, which is not an abstract reality.

Modern ecclesiology has rightly underlined the importance of continuity in the apostolic faith. Continuity remains an essential principle in understanding the history of the church. Orthodox theologians, both before and after 1948, have made a major contribution to the discussions of inner organic catholicity, in the light of which "ecumenism in time" is seen as inseparable from "ecumenism in space". The WCC appeared as a post-World War II event. But its task was not only to heal European and global crises which grew out of the war.

Many voices within the Orthodox community are critical of what is seen as the ecclesiological laxity of the Reformation churches' approach to unity, which systematically bypasses doctrinal divisions, accepts the scandal of division as normal and uncritically justifies the pluralism of confessions by appealing to the diversity of the New Testament.

One way to bypass concern for the "undivided church" is to speculate about the variety of models of unity and of ecumenism. Attention is focussed not on the unifying realities on which "conciliar fellowship" is to be built, but on the recognition of the actual confessional configuration of the churches. No one is ready to make concessions about confessional positions — a reluctance reinforced by the revival of the worldwide expressions of the confessional groups. In the past, many Orthodox argued for a WCC structured as a council of confessional families; and there are still voices today saying that bilateral theological dialogue between confessions must precede multilateral ecumenical dialogue. "Confessionalism", taken for granted in the ecumenical community, prevents the churches from moving towards a sharp vision of unity.

Theologically, the definition of Orthodoxy as the church that preserves the unaltered faith of the seven ecumenical councils (A.D. 325 to 787) raises the question of the so-called "confessional" character of the Orthodox community. But the Orthodox have explicitly rejected this description:

> The Orthodox church possesses its own "confessions" of faith in the forms of creeds and decisions of the ancient councils, especially the ecumenical council. This makes it appear as a "confessional body" or "family" and it is often treated as such by the non-Orthodox. And yet such an understanding of Orthodoxy, sometimes encouraged by the Orthodox themselves, would contradict the fundamental character of its ecclesiology. The Orthodox, if they are faithful to their ecclesiology, will have to deny the identification of the church with a particular confession. A church which is ultimately identified by its "confessions" is a confessional body but not *the* "church." Therefore, in the present form of the World Council of Churches, Orthodoxy constitutes half of the Christian world represented by the Council, and it does so not as one of the "confessional families" of contemporary Christianity, but as the principal tradition of the One Church.[2]

One must be cautious about construing the disunity of Christendom solely in terms of the canonical and cultural estrangement of the two ancient regions, East and West, symbolized by the churches in the two capital cities, Rome and Constantinople. Nicholas Berdyaev supported such a view of "the unity of Christendom in the strife between East and

West."[3] For him the new world epoch could only mean the reunion of East and West — a matter not merely of the churches but of two cultural worlds. The high priority the Orthodox and Roman Catholic Church give to bilateral dialogues with each other is undoubtedly determined by the idea that these two parts of Christianity once constituted an inseparable unit, and that unity means the restoration of that situation.

But the reduction of the ecumenical problem to the schism of 1054 confuses the Body of Christ with past Christendom, and the ecumenical movement with a Christian universalism. For the younger churches in Africa, for example, who know nothing of the Eastern patristic roots of Orthodoxy, the doctrines of the Orthodox Church are only a part of Western theology! One should, therefore, beware of presenting Constantinople and Rome as the two geographical poles of Christendom and their history of schism and reunion as the main subject on the ecumenical agenda.

The weight of past polemics, disputes and anathemas remain heavy. From time to time the "uniatism" which aggravates the links between Orthodox and Catholics and the "proselytism" which disturbs relations with Protestants appear in old and new forms. In terms of ecumenical development, it is also important to point out the ecclesiological regrouping going on within and outside confessional and geographical boundaries. There is now ecclesiological convergence between churches from different cultural and confessional traditions and regions as Christians begin working together and thinking of themselves as communities for others.

Local and universal church

The Orthodox Church focusses its life at both the local and universal levels. The church universal (singular) subsists in local churches (plural). There is no geographical and administrative centre of the church universal, which is a *koinonia* of autocephalous and autonomous local churches. The local church has full catholicity in dogma and liturgy, but has no power to change ecumenical decisions. Among the local churches there is an internal dogmatic unity, sacramental life and eucharistic communion, as well as cultural and national differences.

Orthodox ecclesiology distinguishes between the *unity of the church* and the *unity of churches*. The institutional structures of the various local churches are important, but the union of churches must be based on their unity within the one church, the Body of Christ, the fellowship of the Spirit. The unity of the church does not mean creating a worldwide organization or structure. The one church cannot be realized by putting all the local churches and individual denominations into one global structure. The very existence of local churches, which are not held together by rigid uniformity, confessionalism or jurisdictional centralization, is an evidence of "catholicity".

In fact, ecclesiological debate seems to focus on mutual recognition of the constitutive ecclesiality of the local church. But one of the stumbling blocks to unity is the isolation of the local church — whether out of fear of losing its confessional identity or failure to understand its own proper "catholicity" — from the ecumenical fellowship in its own country or region. The local church is indeed a fully catholic church in a given place, not a fragment or division of some universal, global church. But the local church must be ready to be challenged ecumenically. This raises not only such issues as eucharistic hospitality among various confessional communities, but also solidarity with groups of different races and cultures in the same place. The local church must find some purpose in and encouragement for local ecumenism.

The burgeoning of new forms of Christian community and styles of life and the multiplication of congregations and movements without a clear ecclesial vision often reflect a superficial understanding of ecclesiology. Most sectarian churches with their proselytizing strategy are theologically ambiguous and ecclesiologically anarchical. Meanwhile, from the side of the Roman Catholic Church, one can detect no sign of a decisive concession to the ecclesiology proposed by the Eastern tradition.

Reception by consensus

The Eastern Churches would like to see more reflection on the theological content of unity. Hence their emphasis on the churches' common heritage and tradition. In the WCC, however, the Orthodox are confronted with the dominant Reformation understanding that the New Testament itself witnesses to a great variety of apostolic responses to the gospel, so that many different points of view can claim biblical sanction. Because the New Testament gives evidence of the lack of a unique ecclesiological consensus, Protestant churches insist on reaching a common mind in at least some areas of Christian life, combining various positions and theologies. This implies keeping silent on some doctrinal subjects (because there is no normative authority to appeal to), while acting together on burning issues that demand immediate cooperation. The primary aim of ecumenism comes to be changing attitudes in the internal life of the church; there is no challenge as to how this relates to the experience of the early Christian community.

For the Roman Catholic Church, the question of ecumenical ecclesiology takes a particular form because it affirms a personal focus of unity in the universal church. The pope claims jurisdiction over the universal church not only as successor of Peter as bishop of Rome, but also as vicar of Christ. The First Vatican Council in 1870 formulated the critical doctrine that the pope is infallible *ex sesse*, not *ex consensu ecclesiae*.

The Orthodox, who never conceived the church universal as built on such a personal focus of unity, cannot accept the pope as the final authority in matters of faith and order. The decisions of the First Vatican Council about the claims of the popes of Rome to primacy and supreme authority in the universal church were always rejected by the Eastern patriarchs. Whenever a pope argued on the basis of Matthew 16:19 that he was the successor of Peter, vicar of Christ, the Orthodox pointed to Matthew 18:18, in which all twelve apostles together received the same power and authority. For the Orthodox, the bishop of Rome is the successor of Peter, first among equals, but they cannot agree with the doctrine formulated by the Second Vatican Council (*Lumen Gentium,* 22) that as "Vicar of Christ and pastor of the whole church, the Roman pontiff has full, supreme and universal power over the church". The Eastern Churches built conciliarity around the tradition of the apostolic church, expressed by the synod of bishops of local churches and realized at the level of *consensus fidelium*. A conciliar decision becomes true tradition in its living reception by the full body of Christ.

Many Christians could be willing to accept a leading *pastoral* role for the pope in consideration of the historical position of the bishops of Rome. But this is the only form in which his ministry might be acceptable for all.[4] Communion with the see of the Apostle Peter is not a guarantee of catholicity, but a consequence of it.

Despite the difficulties raised by this particular doctrine of the universality of the church, the Orthodox have regularly raised the issue of Roman Catholic membership in the WCC on the ground that the ecumenical movement cannot ignore this understanding and structure of the universal church. The ecumenical patriarch of Constantinople, Dimitrios I, took up this question during his December 1987 visit to WCC headquarters in Geneva: "We all must be here together," he said.

Regulation of the tradition

For the Orthodox, the content of the apostolic tradition is rooted in the New Testament and was expressed by the church universal during its period of ecumenical consolidation. The Holy Spirit assists the church, which draws its authority from this common apostolic tradition. Various traditions, theological views and liturgical practices may develop in local churches and regional situations, according to historical and sociological factors, but these cannot contradict the basic tradition, which has been preserved to this day.

Such an understanding of tradition implies a regulation of the doctrines or confessions used to carry the apostolic tradition in history; a regulation of the terminology and contextual interpretations as the tradition encounters cultural diversity; a concern for continuity and transmission, because the received tradition is a transmitted word as well as a word to be transmitted.

The tradition is not an independent set of doctrines formulated by a magisterial authority. It includes all the elements of God's revelation which have been received, transmitted and lived in the church under the guidance of the Holy Spirit. In discerning the historical development of the tradition, the episcopate is a sign of the continuity and unity with apostolic times. But although particular attention is given to origins, Pentecost continues in the life of the whole community, which receives the confessions of the synods of the bishops, confirming or challenging the contemporary understanding of their decisions. Here, attention is given to the *chrisma*, the anointing of the Spirit, which gives spiritual illumination to the revelation of God. Through faith, obedience and the indwelling of the Spirit, the people, the "ordinary faithful", have that extraordinary experiential knowledge — *epignosis*.

In fact, the role of the people of God in the mediation of tradition is different today. This is the best illustration of the ecclesiological shift which is necessary, since Orthodox are blocked, as we saw in the previous chapter, between *church-as-model* and *church-as-community*. Idealizing the *church-as-model*, church authority is not eager to validate the people's contemporary experience. The church does not easily allow the faithful to bring their actual prayers and needs into the liturgy. It does not provide a forum for open debate on problems of morality, secularization, family life, political engagement. Internal divisions and crises are misinterpreted, and the sociological reality of women and youth is hidden, because the church is unable to assume them. A critical historical examination is needed of how the tradition affects the identity and unity of the church. The process of *reception* has new elements today.

The questions of authority and ministry have always been linked. Some would confine the teaching church to the magisterium of the ordained ministry, but the Orthodox have always insisted that this authority is not *ex sesse* but *ex consensu ecclesiae*. Authority *in* the church, as a juridical or infallible order, is not to be separated from authority *of* the church, of the people of God who have the spiritual capacity to discern the content of the faith. For the Spirit of God is upon all the baptized, the fullness of the people of God as the bearers of the Spirit.

An inspiring ecumenical model?

The Orthodox cannot accept the loss or distortion of the living reference to the undivided church — the Tradition. They are living out of faithfulness to the tradition of an undivided church. They are conditioned by the common roots of Christianity. They do not spend much time analyzing various views about the tradition. Sometimes they avoid the tensions by keeping at a distance those who have a different point of view.

But a received tradition is a tradition to be transmitted. Therefore, the Orthodox cannot be insensitive to the communication of the tradition today. That requires recovering the space which the tradition has left for imagination and creativity and recognizing that the church is a community of people who make different cultural and pastoral uses of the tradition. No church has a patent on Orthodoxy; each has the right to appropriate the faith according to the needs of its people. In this connection, the Orthodox do distinguish between doctrinal statements *de fide*, which have a binding character, and common opinions. The history of theology, apart from correct views of the Bible and tradition, knows many shortcomings in Bible exegesis and theological interpretations.

The model of unity: eucharistic communion

The visible unity of the church universal is related to the confession of the same faith. Its ultimate expression is the sharing of the same eucharist. The Eastern churches have stated clearly that the broken unity in faith is not a simple matter of theological diversity but something which touches the doctrinal creed, the common confession of faith, and that common reception of the apostolic faith is fundamental in relation to sacramental and eucharistic communion.[5] Full eucharistic communion will not be possible until full unity of faith is achieved. This is the most dramatic and paradoxical dimension of the ecumenical pilgrimage. Several important elements must be taken into account in this process of recognition: the objective reality of confessional diversity, the growing convergence on fundamental doctrines of Christian faith and the urgency of common Christian witness.

In fact, a remarkable degree of agreement on doctrinal matters has been reached. Best known is the effort to achieve ecumenical consensus in the area of *Baptism, Eucharist and Ministry (BEM)*. The consequences of these agreed statements for the unity of the church, especially with respect to eucharistic communion, need further consideration, but there can be no doubt that new entry points have been found into the ecumenical debate, and a growing convergence on the fundamental doctrines of the Christian faith can already be seen.

Concerning eucharistic communion, the Eastern churches have sought not to remain indifferent to those who are not in communion with them and need eucharistic hospitality, while not being pressured into any minimalistic conception of "intercommunion". The debate about "communion" might bring something new to this more restrictive formulation of "the dialectic of openness":

> And yet, our eucharistic openness to the whole does not simply imply that the eucharistic community loses its identity as the chosen and elect Body of Christ. While the eucharistic community itself cuts through all barriers of class and race, of Jew and Gentile, of bond and free, the community has its own integrity, and the unbaptized (including catechumens) are not allowed to share in the eucharist. The eucharist is an act of the community incorporated into Christ by baptism and chrismation. The community opens its doors to the world when the word of God is proclaimed, but closes its doors before it enters the presence of the Almighty where Christ is seated at the right hand of God and where the eucharistic sacrifice is offered eternally by Christ the High Priest.
>
> This dialectic of alternate closing and opening of the doors (of the church, but not of our hearts) is the central mystery of the church's identity and cannot be compromised. Because the table is the Lord's, it does not follow that anyone can indiscriminately partake of the body and blood of the Lord. The eucharist is for the community; the fruit of the eucharistic life is for the world. The eucharist is offered on behalf of the whole creation but only members of the Body of Christ, incorporated into Christ by baptism and chrismation and living his or her life in Christ, can partake of the holy mysteries. None of us are worthy of such participation but God, in his infinite mercy, has made us partakers of the mystery of the eucharist.[6]

But is this a sign that the Orthodox Church is an exclusive community, or is it an awareness of the mystery of the act of eucharistic communion? Nikos Nissiotis's view is this:

> The non-acceptance of inter-communion by the Orthodox in ecumenical gatherings should not be interpreted as a judgement against other churches. It is the expression of an attitude consistent with the fundamental principle that unity is full union and communion. The practice of intercommunion must presuppose this kind of full union or should lead to the immediate abolition of church divisions between those who practice it. The Orthodox, without passing any judgement on those practising intercommunion, play the necessary role for the ecumenical movement of a reminder of the final requirements for re-establishing a full church communion. The rejection of intercommunion by a church like the Orthodox is in the end a rather positive contribution to a realistic, hopeful and authentic vision of the unity to come.[7]

The WCC's Vancouver Assembly spoke about a eucharistic vision of unity — a eucharistic way to live as the church. The eucharist is not just one among the sacraments; it is the sacrament of the people of God in a given place and time, the common food for a scattered pilgrim people. The church must understand itself, its vocation and its mission on the basis of that eucharistic vision. For the eucharist, the *koinonia* in the body and blood of Christ, is the origin of the *koinonia* of Christians as a community of serving and sharing. The churches see their inner unity and solidarity with others as rooted in and related to the Bread of life.

In terms of the prerequisites for eucharistic communion, the practical principles are these:

1. Unity of faith, unity in the doctrine of the undivided church, does not prevent the diversity of legitimate liturgical traditions and eucharistic rites according to churches, cultures and places. Dogmatic imprecisions and canonical disputes which obstruct reciprocal recognition must be the focus for theological dialogue before a unanimous consensus can be reached.

2. Where there is disagreement on the essentials of the faith, there can be no communion in sacraments. The faithful must confess the same faith before sharing the same table and cup. This point can be traced back to the apostolic church, in which fraternal reconciliation was indispensable before bringing the gifts to the altar.

3. Ecclesial *oikonomia* intervenes where the church sees its mission and action for the salvation of persons as requiring an immediate entry point.

NOTES

[1] *Orthodox Contributions to Nairobi*, p.12.
[2] *The Sofia Consultation*, p.69.
[3] The title of his essay in *Ecumenical Review*, I, 1 (1948), 11-24.
[4] John Meyendorff has pointed out that Orthodoxy never denied "that a certain ministry of unity belongs to a 'first bishop'. But this ministry was always understood in moral terms, rather than in terms of formal power or rights." Only when Rome "decisively and consistently pretended to transform its moral 'privilege' into actual jurisdictional and doctrinal power" did the Orthodox East refuse to follow it; "The Council of 381 and the Primacy of Constantinople," in *Le 2e Concile oecuménique* (Chambésy, 1982), p. 410.
[5] Cf. "Intercommunion: An Orthodox Viewpoint," *Ecumenical Review*, X, 4 (1958), 470-74.
[6] *Jesus Christ — the Life of the World*, p.13.
[7] *Orthodox Theological Education*, p.45.

VII. Disputed Issues on the Ecumenical Agenda

Basic orientations

Implicitly or explicitly, certain principles of theological orientation and methodology have been predominant in the history of the WCC. Most member churches perhaps take these for granted, but their dominance can create tensions for a church not structured to follow that line. We may cite three examples:

1. Implicit in the World Council of Churches from the beginning has been an orientation to the stream of Christianity flowing from the Protestant Reformation. The dominance of this spirit can particularly be seen in the understanding of ecclesiological terminology. For this perspective the most challenging issue is: *What is the church?* The Orthodox would never raise that question. They begin from the existence of a united church and then discuss its mission in various places.

Eastern churches are reluctant to accept Reformation principles concerning authority and continuity in the life of the church. The central tension here relates to the existence of different perspectives on unity, which creates the danger that the World Council of Churches presents a plurality of denominational visions of unity, which may even be contradictory.

At best, the two traditions — Reformation and Orthodox — are ignorant of each other. At worst, they engage in stereotyping, with some Reformed dismissing sacred relics and veneration of icons as dry bones and idolatry, and some Orthodox considering a Presbyterian minister (for example) as only a sectarian lay preacher.

2. Another influential stream comes especially from Third World churches, which have developed theologies that take seriously the transforming power of the gospel in social and political history. The WCC's orientation is thus towards the struggle for the rights of the poor and oppressed, bringing them into the liberating purposes of God. Ecumenism and Christian social action are inseparable.

All churches must take seriously the challenge of "liberation theology". And this orientation has indeed inspired many notable changes in the churches' policies and attitudes. But its social philosophy is not completely accepted by many in other traditions. Not all would endorse the emphasis that falls on *action* with the poor to the exclusion of reflection, with the understanding that they express the "prophetic" voice of the church. There are different views of Christian political action and interaction in society, and some churches would insist on a greater focus on personal holiness and liturgical spirituality.

3. Although by definition a "council of churches", the WCC is also an outgrowth of the ecumenical *movement*. Some within the WCC who emphasize the extension of ecumenism among Christians in groups, congregations and movements, ecclesiastical and secular, distinguish between the institutional church and free groups and movements. Questions of ecclesiology are treated as secondary, for the church is seen as one among many sociological communities.

The dominance of "movement" and "congregationalist" positions can lead to bypassing of "the institutional church" or to a view of ecumenism as aimed at changing traditional distinctions, cultural practices and social restrictions which prevent the "institutional" configuration of the church from being the people of God.

Many Orthodox would identify these as negative sides of ecumenism; others would identify such areas of crisis as a focus for constructive interaction between churches of the Reformation traditions and the Orthodox. What the Orthodox cannot accept is having the ecumenism of a given confessional group imposed on them. The Orthodox are loyal to the "catholic" understanding of the church, claiming that their self-expression is more than the ecumenism of a particular church.

At this stage, the answers given by ecumenism are only provisional and partial, but the ecumenical fellowship is strengthened as each church speaks for itself and brings a common vision of unity to the church universal.

A tradition to be recovered

The most critical area is undoubtedly the self-affirmation of confessionalism at the expense of the unity of all. Orthodoxy considers that Western Christianity abandoned the mind of the "catholic" tradition in the process of "confessionalization". What makes the problem of *confessionalism*, which surfaces in different forms, difficult to see is that many persons consider confessional plurality to be the normal status of the ecumenical encounter.

Eastern Christianity would meet the claim which the Reformation made in challenging sixteenth-century Catholicism — that it was rescuing the forgotten tradition through *semper reformanda* and *sola scriptura* — with another claim: *that there **is** a Tradition to be recovered*. The Orthodox antidote to the Reformation tendency to discontinue the flow of the tradition is to go back again and again to the first Christian experience, to "that which was from the beginning" (1 John 1:1). This is the point of reference to which the church must always return, because only by so doing can it gain insights into the heart of the initial apostolic experience, a precious treasure which must be preserved, repeated and renewed. The history of the church is determined by a constant need to be consistent with its origin: "Let that therefore abide in you, which you have heard from the beginning. If that which you have heard from the beginning still remains in you, you also shall continue in the Son and in the Father" (1 John 2:24).

Resolving of the disunity of Christians themselves is thus a matter of appropriating the entire history of the one, holy, catholic and apostolic church. Ecumenical advance in unity is linked to explicit reception of this "catholic" tradition. The common origin of the church universal is not in the Reformation or the Counter-Reformation. The ecumenical movement must understand the history of the church as one dynamic whole.

The Eastern churches, having this global view of history, that is, a perspective on "ecumenism in time", claim to demonstrate the existence of a universal church in history. They insist that the confessional fragmentation and manifold divisions in church history are inconsistent with the unifying action of the one Spirit who spoke by the prophets and acted by the apostles. A superficial reading of church history must be overcome and the methodological tendency to focus on (often-imagined) differences among confessions should be done away with. The churches must always be aware of "the obstinacy of unjustifiable confessional oppositions within the body of Christ" (BEM, *Eucharist*, ch. 20) and ready to renounce these.

In fact, however, there are objective confessional differences among the churches, such as disagreements on the relationship between the Bible and the authority of the church. The biblical notion of *consensus*, of a common tradition of conciliar faith, which is at the heart of ecumenism, has been relativized in the course of history through confessionalism. A predominant view is that there is no single normative ecclesiology or explicit doctrinal consensus on the church in the New Testament. This position, namely the legitimate and necessary diversity in the life of the apostolic and post-apostolic church, finds strong support from recent biblical studies.

This argument is used wrongly by those who claim that the differences in the New Testament correspond to the confessional and structural divisions imposed by Christian experience in history. When "conciliarity" is based on the idea that there is a plurality of Christologies and ecclesiologies and that Scripture does not allow for the formulation of "consensus", there will always have to be an intermediate step, a middle term, on the way to unity, but no expectation of full consensus. The consequence is a retreat from ecumenical discussion of controversial issues, a deep disquiet that the churches cannot reach a "consensus" and a recognition that Christian unity is still too partial and fragile to sustain a radical confrontation.

But confessional identity has recently taken on new dimensions. The dividing lines among the churches, especially in mission, social ethics and diakonia, are not defined exclusively by confessional criteria but run across the churches. Even theologically, the old stereotype of an unbridgeable gulf between Reformation churches, with their priority on the proclamation of the Word and the doctrine of Holy Scripture as the only norm of authority, and the churches of the "Catholic" stream, with their insistence on *tradition*, understood as the total life of the historical church, is formulated today in a positive way. Bible and tradition are no longer seen as divergent entities, giving two contradictory responses.

Theology and spirituality of the here-and-now

Orthodox churches also perceive a danger in the excesses of contextualization and what might be called "messianic activism". By definition a "council of churches", the WCC, in pursuing unity, has often adopted the methodology of a "movement", focussing on concepts and insights that make sense for a particular period of history. The Orthodox are uncomfortable with this methodology, because it gives priority to provisional achievements, interim practical steps and contextual expressions of unity, while forgetting the "old crisis". Those who accent the "movement" aspect of the WCC observe that it is not always doctrines which separate Christians but attitudes and history; therefore, ecumenism must be relevant to the daily life of believers and the human community. The Orthodox argue that some confessional and contextual paraphrases of the gospel could become heretical.

This is not to deny that the pastoral aspect of the "movement" is also meaningful for the Orthodox. They do not limit the WCC to a closed organization or institution. There is a general lack of ecumenical enthusiasm in the churches, because people find theological dialogue too formal, ignoring the dimension of pastoral care and spirituality. What the Orthodox ought to do in analyzing the movement is to regard the visible and invisible aspects in the same light. In order to be in a movement we need, if not consensus, at least an appropriation of common convictions. We need a common vision. This implies reassessment of the ecumenical situation as a continuous process.

In spite of all the divisive issues, the ecumenical climate is positive. All churches have stated clearly that the ecumenical movement is an irreversible process. In this positive climate, the churches should respect the diversity of the particular missions Christians have had in history and cannot abandon. They should recover a sense of the urgency of joint action in such vital issues as the struggle for economic justice, the suffering of the oppressed, racism, violence. Avenues for the ecumenical participation of movements, groups and networks should be opened in the search for unity and renewal of the human community. The churches should move to a new stage in their quest for visible unity by mutual recognition of their ministries, common acceptance of each other's baptism and extension of eucharistic hospitality.

Ecclesiological perceptions of each other

A crucial ecumenical question is that of the criteria for explicit recognition of each other's baptism, eucharist and ministry. For the Orthodox the question is this: What is the basis for affirming the ecclesial nature of Protestant congregations?

Central to the issue of common recognition is the evaluation of each other's doctrine of ordained ministry and of the forms in which this ministry is exercised. The theme of ministry, of course, raises the issue of the source and structures of authority. Painful as it may be, the ecumenical debate on structures of power and authority for building up of the body which facilitate or hinder the participation of all is unavoidable. An illustration of how difficult this discussion is came at the WCC's sixth assembly (1983), when a remark made by the general secretary that authority may be misused in the church was immediately construed in some quarters as an attack on the hierarchical priesthood.

In the eucharist the church celebrates the great mystery of the salvation of humanity, the final destiny of the world. Ecclesiastically divided groups of Christians are not sharing the same eucharist. While there is a new ecumenical awareness of the important implications of the eucharist for unity, the canonical disciplines for eucharistic hospitality and sharing are not commonly recognized, apart from experiments which, instead of facilitating unity, create more problems. The Orthodox formulate conditions of ecclesiality and sacramentality in very specific — and sometimes too restrictive — terms.

The possibility of a formal recognition of each other's eucharist as the sacrament of our unity in the Body of Christ must be explored, although any such recognition will depend on other factors. Consensus on ministry is connected with the content of the church's faith.

The practice of ecumenical worship is confusing to the Orthodox. But there is an element of universality in their own worship which should be explored further, both in terms of the offering of eucharistic communion to others and in terms of the struggle from outside, where the community can operate in overcoming internal divisions. For the disciplined worshipping community has the capacity not only to manifest its identity and loyalty, but also to transcend these and to be in solidarity with others. In some situations, the Orthodox liturgy can have a profoundly symbolic ecumenical value, precisely for those who are not able to celebrate and to receive the bread of life. In such situations, the community may be opened to offer the eucharist to those who are in need. Where there is bread and wine, changed by the Holy Spirit into the body and blood of the incarnated and risen Christ, there are no borders. The Spirit compels that these be shared with those who are poor and oppressed, under the power of sin and injustice, whether at home or far away in places unpenetrated by the grace of the Lord. The discipline of eucharistic communion and openness must be challenged from *inside*, in the name of the solidarity of the church with the world.

Renewal: the faith of the church, not our sins

The relation between unity and renewal is an essential aspect of contemporary ecumenical spirituality. The church is a community of penitents who, recognizing the brokenness and weakness of their own lives, struggle to live in communion with God in a liturgical fellowship and to serve the world in Christ's way. But the God-given holiness of the church does not mean that it need not be concerned about *renewal*. For the church has to ask itself whether it is really an *oikoumene* where people can indeed have a new vision of history and the experience of being a new community around the Risen Lord. The struggle for renewal has to do with the essential nature of the church as *basileia* while living in human history.

The spirituality of renewal is an experience that takes Christians to a reality beyond themselves, to God's fullness in himself, to the depth of the death and life of Jesus Christ. Renewal means bringing into reality the life in Christ which is granted to every Christian in baptism. It calls for a process of sanctification which goes to the limit, to the condition of the cross, to a heroic combat until Christ is fully formed in us.

It is true that the institutional image of the church has been abused in the history of Christendom. Its historical reality sometimes stands in sharp contrast to its proclamation and mission. There is a gulf between church-as-symbol and church-as-community. The ambiguous history of the church cannot avoid confusing people. In recent decades, awareness of these aspects has surfaced: the sin of institutionalism, the temptation to sacralize false powers and authorities through various forms of social change and liberation movements. But despite the sins and betrayals of its members, the church remains faithful to its Lord through those who are faithful. Because of them, Christians can humbly confess that their community, as repentant and pardoned sinners, presents the Reign of God, which has come and is coming, to the world.

The coming of the Holy Spirit to change the broken bread into the Body of Christ is the only way to heal the brokenness of the community. The eucharist is at the heart of the renewed community insofar as it becomes real food: for the poor, a symbol of dispossession; for women, a symbol of powerlessness; for children, a symbol of defenselessness. The eucharist itself is therefore the dynamic heart of the ecclesial community in which both men and women find their consecration and unity.

Clouds of theologies and ecclesiologies

One of the priorities which the Sixth Assembly (Vancouver, 1983) formulated for the work of the World Council of Churches was *Vital and Coherent Theology*. The assembly recognized the many theological, social and methodological issues which create ambiguities and tensions in ecumenical life and work. The WCC has no authority to resolve these in a magisterial way, but in the course of debating these the Council needs to provide a frame of reference for all, in order to arrive at common theological convictions and spiritual insights. The WCC has spoken in terms of a "holistic approach" and a "eucharistic vision", but it has not worked out a specific methodology for keeping theologically divisive issues and programmes together in a positive tension. It should be noted that the Orthodox have not paid much attention to this subject, so that "Protestant" voices became predominant in the WCC, creating the impression that the Council had no other theological methodology.

At least two main methodologies are in permanent tension in the ecumenical dialogue.

One is a "catholic" view, which might be described as an "ontological" vision of unity. This is concerned primarily with mediating the fullness of the faith and experience of the church since its origin, not only in its historical and contemporary setting, but also in terms of coherence between doctrine, spirituality and worship. This understanding is expressed in the terminology of "apostolic succession", which tries to keep a balance between Scripture and Tradition, apostolic faith and contemporary experience. The Pentecost community continues, and the Holy Spirit is the sustainer of this extension of the time of the gospel.

This understanding underlines the factual, institutional reality of the church and suspects the Reformation of interrupting the continuity if not altering the reality of the whole. The centre from which to judge all of history, the prophetic witness, the New Testament and the apostolic tradition is Jesus Christ, who sent his Holy Spirit to edify the people of God — the church having already been foreseen by the prophets and originating in his incarnation and resurrection.

The other methodology is a "Reformation" view, which we might call a "vocational" vision of unity. This seems to "break" the apostolic succession, with its primary concern for the immediate personal practice of the gospel, for historical responses and for provisional values which serve the immediate context. It has less concern for the totality of the tradition, lived according to the teaching of the Holy Scriptures as the only authority for the faith.

It should be noted that the Reformation, in its criticism of Western Catholicism, did not rely methodologically on the Eastern tradition. Its basic principle, *semper reformanda*, liberates the church from a traditional point of reference in order to articulate "confessional" statements in history to serve specific missions and tasks. Its attitude towards authority, ecclesiastical or theological, is liberal, criticizing institutional forms as always relative and provisional. The key hermeneutical principle is fulfillment by the power of the Holy Spirit. Pentecost continues, but it is manifested as a "crisis" that surprises and changes history.

Can these divergent views, which seem to suggest two different visions of unity — one *ontological* and another *vocational* — be reconciled?

First we should look at the positive elements in each of them. The logic of the "catholic" or "ontological" trend requires accepting not only diversity but also "crisis" in the development of Christendom, and in specific missions of particular people in the *oikoumene*, which is larger than the visible Eastern community. In the same way, the logic of the "Reformation" or "vocational" trend requires overcoming the ethical and "missionary" attitude and having a unifying principle and a point of reference for the essentials of the Christian faith.

Therefore, the ecumenical "vision" is developed from two logics. Some would say that the ecumenical movement is an historical and pastoral necessity but not an ontological ecclesial condition, since Orthodoxy has a *unity* in its own right. It is better to say that the ecumenical commitment of the Eastern churches emerges from both within and outside the inner life of the church, from both its being and vocation.

Second, ecumenism offers a large space for dialogue and encounter among confessions, schools of theology, hermeneutical approaches, cultures, intellectual perceptions and metaphysics, provided that there is a discipline of dialogue accepted mutually.

All churches have the right to voice their own particular ecclesiology and to articulate what they see as appropriate ways to seek unity; but definitions which portray other churches *a priori* in a false light must be abandoned, as well as obstinate exaggeration of "unjustifiable confessional opposition" by extreme dogmatic positions. There is an ongoing process of "reception", which signifies not only accepting what is legitimate diversity but also rejecting what seems to be an obstacle to unity. There is a capacity to recognize and evaluate objectively new ecumenical experiences as building blocks which may overcome some of the traditional divisions and disputes. And above all, there is a "dialogue of love" which, according to the Ecumenical Patriarch Athenagoras, constitutes the essence of Christian integrity. [1]

What are the main issues leading to persistent ambiguities, confusions and tensions need to be examined seriously in a common theological framework of reference?

The ecumenical movement will not be relevant for the Orthodox if the central issue of their confession — the *theological content of the unity and witness of the church* — is not on the agenda. This includes a series of subjects: the authority of Scripture in relation to the variety of confessional traditions and doctrinal views; the articulation of the faith, that is, how the church formulates its own deepest truths and insights in order to maintain its visible unity; the ways of teaching authoritatively, and the vocabulary used to express distinctive positions.

The most critical issue is the *vision* of the ecumenical process to unity. At any moment, this can break the fellowship into ecclesiastical camps. Thus the WCC should keep a sharp focus on unity and on theological language. Ecumenical optimism based on the idea of reuniting confessional bodies originating in the sixteenth century is no longer valid. Their rigid confessionalism makes *reception* impossible, although the Orthodox recognize in them several essential elements of the permanent tradition of the church. Next to them are the charismatic, Pentecostal and evangelical movements, groups and voluntary associations, all claiming to have something to say in terms of unity. It is difficult for the Orthodox to evaluate their ecclesial status or to speak about recognizing them as sister churches.

Another ambiguity is over the way the local experience reflects or obscures the ecumenical climate established at the international level. The local situation is often the shadow zone of ecumenism. We must encourage an appropriate local ecumenical experience and a serious theological appreciation of it.

Finally, the Orthodox fear reducing the great movement for visible unity to the solidarity of Christians in some area of human concern. But they recognize the urgency of the common Christian witness now possible and the actual practice of it.

Community of women and men in the church

Many of the issues taken up in this exceptional study, which culminated in the Sheffield Consultation (1981), are now being considered within the context of the *Ecumenical Decade of Churches in Solidarity with Women*. To introduce the Ecumenical Decade, the WCC indicated a preliminary agenda and a working framework.[2] There are, of course, areas in which further clarification is needed if churches from different political situations and theological traditions are to sustain and translate into action the purposes of the Decade — especially the basic theological positions. "Feminist theology" may be an entry point for some, but it can erode ecumenical solidarity if it excludes others from formulating their own theological approaches.[3] During the Ecumenical Decade, the churches should be asked which theological positions they want to *confirm*, to *challenge*, to *promote*. There has been a serious attempt in the Decade to appropriate new theological insights into ecumenical experience: particularly the resurrection as a basis for change (women are compared with "a growing stream of resurrection people") and the trinitarian understanding of God as a basis for the solidarity within the community.

In ecumenical reflection, the interpretation of the Bible and the understanding of church history from the perspective of women must be submitted to certain criteria. Often, contradictions between the gospel and the tradition of the church are taken for granted, and the subordination or oppression of women is simplistically attributed to church doctrine. Some of the "theses" of feminist theology are anti-biblical; and those who claim to preserve the tradition of the early church do not accept a liberal view about the history of the church.

However, an analysis of actual experiences and situations is needed. The idolatrous power structures which oppress women must be identified; and the obstacles to women's full and active participation in church and society must be removed. But these structures and obstacles are not the same everywhere. The secularization of the church and politicization of society vary from one country to another. "Hierarchical structures" have different meanings in different ecclesiologies. The Decade must be sufficiently open to cope with a multiplicity of contextual and ecclesial options. What implications does the new emphasis on an "ecclesiology of communion" have on solidarity with women?

Theological issues like the authority of the church and in the church, ordination of women, structures and patterns of leadership and ministry must be approached in an ecumenically responsible way. Especially the way in which the issue of the ordination of women is formulated must be acceptable to all.

Here the churches can easily declare the issue a "matter of faith" on which no theological convergence is possible. The debate in Vancouver, alluded to earlier, about the exercise of power and use of authority in the church showed that these issues are subject to many misinterpretations and misunderstandings. The purpose of the Ecumenical Decade is not to force churches into theological concessions but to change cultural practices and social restrictions which have no ground in the Christian faith.

The Ecumenical Decade could mark an important development of ecumenical convictions and perspectives at the end of this millennium. But the WCC is well aware of how divisive and frustrasting such a programme may become at any time. The Ecumenical Decade needs a broad and solid foundation in order to move the ecumenical community to a new degree of organic unity.

An excellent affirmation of the Orthodox position on "Women in the World and the Church" was made by an inter-Orthodox consultation on *Orthodox perspectives on creation* (Sofia, 1987):

> Both in personal attitudes and in institutional life, the world has a long history during which women have been unjustly treated, and their essential humanity as God's image and likeness has not been fully respected. Such sinful divisiveness is not acceptable from an Orthodox Christian perspective (cf. 1 Cor. 11:11). In the world re-created by Christ, both male and female dimensions are integrally related to each other (cf. Gal. 3:28). The genuine harmony between these two dimensions is a symbol of the integrity of creation in its diversity. We Orthodox must recommit ourselves to the truth of our faith according to which women's true dignity is as "joint heirs to the grace of life" (cf. 1 Pet. 3:7) existing together with men. We must raise in our consciousness the important affirmation of our faith that, as members of the Body of Christ, women share in the "royal priesthood" (cf. 1 Pet. 2:9) of all believers. It is of fundamental importance in the Orthodox church that a woman became the mother of our Incarnate Saviour and that she remains the model *par excellence* of the integral humanity to which all Christians, men and women, aspire. Historically, we have always recognized in the church the diaconal (cf. Rom. 16:1; 1 Tim. 5:9-10), witnessing (cf. Mt. 28:10) and nurturing roles of women (cf. 2 Tim. 5:9-10). In particular, Orthodox men must acknowledge that, as full members of the church, women share in the intercessory vocation of the church to stand in the presence of the Lord on behalf of all creation. In concrete terms we must find means to allow the considerable talents of women in the church to be devoted as fully as possible in the Lord's service for the building up of the kingdom. This means more opportunities for theological education for women and the opening of career opportunities in the church for women. Serious consideration must be given to the re-introduction of the ancient order of Deaconess by the hierarchies of the local churches. [4]

Uniatism

Recent events in the Ukraine and elsewhere have raised the problem of uniatism in all its dimensions. Among "disturbing trends" mentioned by the WCC Central Committee in a March 1990 statement on developments in Central and Eastern Europe was "the attempts to revitalize the Union of Brest-Litovsk of 1596". The reference to this 400-year old event, no doubt unfamiliar to most Protestants, was an invitation to learn something critical about the history of the churches in countries where uniatism was introduced to force their absorption into Catholicism, destroying their integrity and identity.

Confessionally speaking, *uniatism* allows Eastern churches to preserve their synodical and liturgical diversity while acknowledging the person and role of the Bishop of Rome as the centre of visible universal unity. On this basis, Rome has succeeded in creating Western "Catholic" parallels to all Eastern and Oriental Orthodox churches. Their existence disfigures the image of both Orthodoxy and Catholicism. Through uniatism, Latin popes created an artificial Western Christianity in the midst of the most ancient apostolic churches, such as Jerusalem and Antioch, and of the most large and popular churches such as the Russian and Romanian churches. The Greek Catholic churches have now been recognized as a branch of Latin Christianity, but the Orthodox cannot forget the humiliation they suffered from this in the past.

Historically, uniatism was built on a falsification of the history of the Eastern churches, which led to fierce persecution of the Orthodox by Western political powers. To justify the conversion of "separated Eastern brothers" in the Balkan countries, for example, it was said that Christianity there was of Latin origin; in fact, Orthodoxy was introduced by missionaries in the ninth century.

It is not surprising that the Pope, in formulating the Latin view on European Christianity, has taken this method and practice for granted. But he also knows that the Orthodox will not allow their history and ecclesiology to be trifled with. They can prove that the actual expansion of papal authority in the East was built on the falsification of history; and once this is recognized, the *raison d'être* of papal primacy and jurisdiction in the East will disappear.

Although uniatism is being propagated in many ways, the Orthodox are condemning it as a counter-witness more strongly now than in the past. One reason for this is that European Christianity needs a tradition of reference which provides a deep sense of catholicity as the work of the Holy Spirit. Emphasis on the spirit of catholicity or universality as communion in the Spirit questions the validity of the Roman Catholic theory of "the two lungs". This theory may be attractive as an aid for understanding the formation of two distinctive traditions in Christianity after A.D. 1054. But can it serve as a legitimate working hypothesis for ecumenical dialogue in Europe today? Can we rest content with the establishment of two parts of Christianity, East and West? History has created this situation of division. Through territorial and cultural restrictions it concretely affected the mission of the Eastern churches. But the Orthodox, behind their limited territorial existence, have always had the mind of the undivided "catholic" church, which is an historical way "to preserve the unity of the Spirit in the bond of peace" (Eph. 4:3).

A second reason for the renewed reaction of the Orthodox on the uniate issue has to do with the question of Orthodox identity. The uniates cannot replace the Orthodox in their involvement in European Christianity. The Orthodox cannot delegate this mission to others. They reject the argument that old and new uniatism is an organic link between the East and the West — not only because the Orthodox church is now a missionary church (as the large diaspora in the West demonstrates), but also because the West must know the Orthodox directly, not via another tradition.

The Orthodox have always challenged universal uniatism as a model of the unity of the Christian churches.

NOTES

[1] Olivier Clément, "Athenagoras I: Orthodoxy in the Service of Unity," *Ecumenical Review*, XXV (1973), 310-28.

[2] See *Ecumenical Review*, XL, 1 (Jan. 1988), with articles by Emilio Castro, Pauline Webb, Chung Hyun-Kyung, Janet Crawford, Thomas Best and Una Kroll.

[3] Cf. "An Orthodox Response," in Frederick R. Wilson, ed., *Your Will Be Done : Mission in Christ's Way* (Geneva: WCC, 1990), pp. 185f., particularly on the issues of "tampering with the language of the Bible" and the ordination of women to the priesthood.

[4] Cf. also "Women in the Church," in *Orthodox Contributions to Nairobi*, p.33, which notes that "while the Orthodox churches are making fairly intense efforts to make it possible for women to share more fully in ecclesial life, they tend to yield to specific request rather than take any steps to re-examine the problem as a whole".

VIII. Orthodoxy:
A Matter of Relevance

What relevance does the Orthodox witness have for the ecumenical community at the end of the twentieth century? How do the Eastern churches confirm or challenge the main trends in ecumenical ecclesiological thought? What is their vision of ecumenism today and tomorrow?

Focus on unity

Eastern Christians believe and pray for unity in the likeness of the holy trinitarian God, abiding in three persons united in their distinction and distinct in their unity. Hence in the mystery of the church there is a sense of the communion of God and of the wholeness of creation.

In his incarnation and resurrection, Jesus Christ *Pantokrator* embraces all of humanity and the creation. The church, his body, should radiate from within itself the cosmic power of his cross and resurrection. The catholicity of the church is thus something more and deeper than the mere universality of Christendom.

The building up of an *ecclesia* — the Body of Christ, people of God — is inherent in the logic of the gospel of love. It is a prefigured *basileia*, a new creation in our midst. It is not a branch of a confessional body, a society or a voluntary organization. It is not an illusion but a reality, the people of God, the people of the New Testament, sent and consecrated to praise the Father, to remember and recognize the Son, to invoke the Holy Spirit for the sanctification of all.

The theology of the Holy Spirit as the divine person who communicates glorifying "divine energies" at the personal and communal levels liberates the church from a closed, static, transcendent model of spiritual life. Everyone who is sanctified participates directly and personally in one and the same Holy Spirit, the Spirit of freedom. In sending his Spirit, Jesus Christ called people to full freedom, to personal conversion and to reconciliation as a community.

Orthodox avoid scholastic terminology in communicating the articles of faith, preferring an organic language and terminology. Their theology draws heavily on mystical and liturgical experience.

Although a church with a hierarchical priesthood, the Orthodox venerate the charismatic "ordinary people", for they are the ones who finally preserve the faith and incarnate it in life.

Equally the Orthodox emphasize the unity of the local and of the universal church, because they believe in the "catholic" nature and eucharistic character of each local church.[1] Their emphasis on the church as *communion* of the baptized and anointed, with a new reality, visible and invisible, is extremely important. Unity at the universal level is conceived as a conciliar unity, implying full communion among all local churches in faith, sacraments and order. Each local church is recognized as part of the whole church, belonging to all times and all places.

There is also a communion or consensus among various canonical authorities — local bishops, local and regional synods — which is expressed at the universal level by the ecumenical synod. It originates in apostolic practice: "for it seemed good to the Holy Spirit and to us" (Acts 15:28). The primacy of the bishop of Rome is also subject to conciliarity. It is a ministry which has an historical reality and a canonical configuration, but it has no jurisdiction or authority over the universal church, which is not a worldwide organization but a fellowship of local churches.

The Orthodox claim to be a community with an apostolic, patristic, ecumenical legacy. They witness to the common understanding of the tradition of origin: "the faith which was once delivered to the saints" (Jude 3). Traditions are not only historical, contextual responses, but ways for each local church to receive and live the common tradition. There is a conciliar way both to test the faithfulness of each local church and to receive diverse traditions and cultures.

Why should one be specifically "Orthodox" in certain doctrines? Because Orthodox believe that Pentecost continues as a revelation of the Spirit in community, which carries on the history that constitutes the content, mind and purpose of the initial Christian experience. Their confession emerges out of apostolic tradition and a struggle against heretical expressions and speculations. For this reason, the Orthodox will always insist on being part of the ecumenical theological dialogue on traditional doctrines.

An ecumenical "canon"?

In a time when the churches remain divided and weak, in an unstable world where so many nations and people are troubled by poverty and insecurity, to reaffirm the urgency of a healthy ecumenical life is not just a spiritual obligation but common sense. For it would be absurd to fragment anew the hard-won "conciliar fellowship" Christians have reached or to give up existing unity as futile. Consolidating the elements which have created a basis for entering into a preconciliar process, the ecumenical movement must be both sober and bold in the search for unity.

The World Council of Churches must continue the effort to sharpen the understanding of the nature of conciliar fellowship and to make known new experiences of its conciliar life. At various occasions, it has spoken of the "visible unity" of divided churches (1954), of "our oneness in Christ and our disunity as churches" (1954), and of "conciliar fellowship" (1975). Yet the three terms in the title of the Central Committee's Toronto Statement (1950) — *Church, the churches and the council of churches* — are not yet clarified. The question of the ecclesiological significance of the WCC is related to these.

1. The ecclesiological debate must advance into a new phase. In the 1950s, the World Council of Churches made very clear that it is not a substitute for the church or a "super-church". It is not the manifestation of the one church, nor does it deny the individual identities, confessional doctrines or institutional status of its members. The objections to giving "ecclesiological significance" to the Council arose mainly from the false idea that the Council aspired to become a "super-church".[2]

But the recent positive experiences of unity as "conciliar fellowship" need to be made more explicit. The churches have taken significant steps from ecclesiastical "estrangement" towards a fuller common ecclesial life. *Baptism, Eucharist and Ministry*, a document of remarkable ecumenical convergence built on common ecclesiological grounds, substantiates this process and is a preparation for fuller unity. Moving the debate about ecclesiological significance beyond generalities and freeing it from the "super-church" complex means asking very specifically: What kind of communion is possible? What is the *content* of this conciliar fellowship of churches on the way, which gives signs of unity? Closed ecclesiological and confessional systems which sometimes use the ecumenical movement as a forum to legitimate themselves, must be challenged. An ecumenism that responds to today's pastoral needs is indispensable, but it must not replace the struggle for an appropriate ecclesiological restoration or it could serve to actualize the disunity and fragmentation.

2. The churches must help the WCC to go beyond the simple language of credibility when it explains its rationale. Western Protestantism has argued inductively for the unity of the church in the interest of mission in and service to the world for whom the church exists. The Orthodox see this as a lack of sensitivity to the scandal of division, tolerating disunity in the church as a given. Unity belongs to the essence of the church; it is not an optional fringe benefit. We confess one holy church, one people of God, not only to enable a united credible witness, but because the church is called to be *basileia* — the glorified sign and instrument of the fundamental unity of all which is given in Jesus Christ. The churches must proclaim and live this one profound reality, without a complex about giving visible, "credible" signs.

A tension exists between those who focus on the "identity" of an established entity which maintains the integrity of the community, and those who accent "credibility" — the community's function of giving a credible Christian witness. For the former, unity may appear as a "threat", because it can push the community to become disloyal to a particular tradition and to revise basic theological assumptions. For the latter, there is a fear that a community which does not respond immediately to a need may become disobedient to the gospel.

Such false distinctions can derail ecumenism. What is required to strengthen and enrich the community is both greater faithfulness to the tradition and greater obedience to the gospel on the part of the members. Indeed, the activism of some members can split the community, either because they become impatient with the slow pace of the rest of the community, or because they are consistently marginalized.

3. The ecumenical movement has overemphasized the role of the church's institutional shortcomings in causing both the unbelief of the world and the historical divisions of the church. Moreover, an ethos of tension gives the impression of being in entrenched positions, of remaining in intrinsic "estrangement" and perpetual conflict. The assumption that there have always been divisions and disagreements in church history, which should be tolerated as objective confessional differences, implies that the World Council of Churches considers that theological method may contradict the objective truth received in the tradition of the New Testament, for example: "We have the fellowship with Jesus Christ" (1 John 1:6).

4. It is extremely frustrating for the Orthodox when ecumenical dialogue does not allow them to say and manifest what they are, even at the level of methodology.

Theological methodologies, sometimes very contradictory, constitute one of the pitfalls of contemporary ecumenism. "Integrists" will ask: how much diversity in doctrine, moral teaching and witness will promote the confession of the one faith in the one church? "Confessionalists" will say: there is a permanent, insurmountable contradiction between the historical realities and confessional responses on one hand and the eschatological vision of truth on the other. The Orthodox would claim that it is high time to revise this methodology of tension and contradiction and recover the language of mutual acceptance, recognition and reception. The process of reception could become a healthy dynamic for moving beyond historical "estrangement" to affirming the common ground given to all.

This will be an immense task, obliging the churches to deal with deep differences in their categories of thought and expression. But the Orthodox are not persuaded by facile arguments for confessionalism and contextualism which speak of "creative tension" among the various confessional expressions of the Christian faith and different social, political and cultural contexts. They call for serious theological work to recognize the "canon", the common norm coming from the apostles, in all streams of church life, all spiritual and theological currents which seek to express the gospel and live it more relevantly in various contexts. What do we hold to be the content of apostolic faith — which is the ground of unity — in all confessional and contextual ecclesiologies? The Orthodox see the persistence of closed confessional systems as a sign that the churches are unwilling to think anew about the growing of their ecclesial reality and their freedom from systems in the perspective of the fullness of the tradition.

5. A word about the liturgical context of the World Council of Churches.[3] The Vancouver assembly (1983) showed not only that common worship offers immense potential for a conciliar fellowship among churches, but also that the WCC cannot be understood apart from its continued prayers, mutual intercessions, sharing of spiritualities and eucharistic communion.

All churches agree that the eucharist is the centre of the liturgical life, that the sacramental celebration of faith has the same value as the proclamation of the word and social responsibility in the world; and all acknowledge the obstacles still hindering eucharistic communion. The Orthodox make it clear that eucharistic communion expresses full unity in faith and sacramental life (Romans 1:12) and that in the present situation of "real, but incomplete communion" it would thus be a deceptive gesture to offer eucharist without discernment.

But how far could the evolution of conciliar life constitute a basis for the Orthodox to adopt the practice of *oikonomia* in this matter? In the interest of affirming theological convergences in the apostolic faith, of empowering Christians to be organs of peace and justice in a divided world, of consolidating the experience of common witness and of healing past divisions, can the eucharistic communion become a means both to express and to achieve a true conciliar life? Of course, a common eucharist is not a way of forcing common recognition of other sacraments and ministries without sufficient preparation for this. Could the eucharist be shared not only to consolidate a proper ecclesial life and celebrate the reunion of divided Christians, but also to challenge exclusive, historically organized communities to transcend their visible institutional limits in order to share the "common bread and cup" in a more catholic way, with others and for others who need the bread of life? Some Orthodox think that there is a possible immediate eucharistic communion among the churches that have maintained the historic episcopacy, based precisely on the understanding of eucharist as a foretaste of *basileia*, as an *end* to division in Christianity and the world.

Appearances and depths

More than forty years after Amsterdam, the difficult problems raised by the Orthodox require more time for dialogue. Indeed, the mélange of visions of ecumenism in the WCC and throughout the ecumenical movement create vagueness about objectives and strategies. The resulting confusion obstructs internal dialogue and mutual recognition. For some the concept of visible unity may imply the universality of Christianity via communion with Rome; for others, it implies solidarity with Christians in situations of urgent need; for others, it is a matter of the orthodoxy of faith, life and order and of consistency with the origin and historical development of the church. These contrasting meanings attached to ecumenism should be submitted to the standard of the church's "calling to unity in communion", which has its integrity. This is to recognize and to live Christ as it has been confessed in the beginning and yesterday, as it must be lived today and tomorrow for the glory of God and the renewal of all creation.

Under the pressure of the Orthodox, the WCC must take seriously, in all its talk about Christian unity and church identity, the theological reference point of the ecumenical movement. The responsibility here lies primarily with those who multiply without limit the ecumenical challenges, to whom the Orthodox reply before any debate; with those who feel uncomfortable about theological questions, preferring ethical and social considerations; with those who increase the differences and tensions.[4] If the World Council of Churches fails to grasp this challenging moment, the Orthodox will be pushed into further frustration. Finally, it is not only a matter of taking a responsible position, but also of the Council's achieving a more comprehensive understanding of itself and its integrity.

It seems that the role of the Eastern churches is precisely to make possible at least two prerequisites of the ecumenical movement: to uphold the apostolic roots of the church universal, and to associate the "focus of unity" in the movement with the identity of the church in the full richness of its diversity. The church universal is rooted in confessing the apostolic faith that surrounds the Pentecost community, and in living this apostolic faith together (though in particular traditions and ways). Thus, there is in the ecumenical movement a multiplicity of options, a heterogeneity of streams and forces which may threaten its integrity and prevent the people from seeing clearly the "focus of unity", namely the common identity of the church expressed in the common eucharist. The Orthodox themselves (who have allowed room for secondary elements in the expression of Orthodoxy and whose labyrinth of public worship and canonical digressions does not help the people to grasp that central focus) should visualize that possible vision of unity in order to shed new light on the identity of the church in its fullness.

There should be something in common among ecclesiological reflection, self-examination of the history of the church and ecumenical spirituality. It has been said that it is sometimes difficult for the Orthodox to recognize others as full churches within the fellowship of the WCC. In spite of that, we live with what Nikos Nissiotis called "a scandalous mystery", because there is "something paradoxical in the consistent Orthodox theological involvement in the ecumenical movement". For him, this ecumenical paradox is related to an ecclesiological paradox: "the contradictory reality of the Church existing as churches". At Vancouver it was said again: "There can be no churches (in the plural), except as manifestations of the one true Church (in the singular)." The World Council of Churches dramatizes this paradox, because it can be interpreted as a federation of *churches* without concern for the identity of *the* one Church. While Orthodox accept this paradox as part of their faith, they are aware of the mystery behind their own communion, the mystery of the revelation and grace of God who embraces in the power of the Holy Spirit all humanity and creation.

"The divine Grace that heals every weakness and supplies whatever is lacking" (*The prayer of ordination*) — the power of the Holy Spirit — takes hold of Christians and leads them where God wills. The present and the future belong to the Spirit, for the Spirit of God has not abandoned the church or the world. Despite human unbelief and disobedience, God is at work. But this does not justify our failures, for our lack of love hinders the Spirit. The Spirit helps us in our weakness, but weakness remains weakness if there is no repentance and faith:

> Our problem today is that we are so preoccupied with our past failures and present powerlessness that we do not set our minds on the Spirit of God, who is wise and powerful. So long as we put our trust in our own wisdom and resources, the Spirit of God does not do his mighty acts through us. "We have this treasure in earthen vessels, to show that the transcendent power belongs to God and not to us" (2 Cor. 4:7). That transcendent power is not limited by our limitations, but only waits for our repentance and faith to receive that power.[5]

Orthodox assets

1. The Eastern churches have a great capacity for seeing the ecumenical movement and the search for visible unity in the context of the total history of Christianity. Of course, the churches are confronted by the world's needs and must respond to them, but they are also confronted by the wider picture of ecumenical Christianity. Now Orthodox history carries the age and the spirit of Christianity. This historical perspective is not a simple problem of a return to the ancient traditions but an understanding of the "catholic" nature of Christianity.

Perhaps the Orthodox do not have an adequate method to respond to present historical times, but they can affirm that there is a given visible unity at Pentecost. Out of the historical experience of this, they have a perception of unity that is imaginable by and for all.

2. Another asset of the Orthodox is their confidence in a tradition which is not merely a collection of doctrines, creeds and confessional or liturgical books, but a chain of witnesses who committed themselves — concrete names and experiences, events such as the ecumenical councils of bishops, and witnesses such as saints, confessors and martyrs. The "clouds of witnesses" have the same experience in various times and places.

Apostolic succession was preserved not by eliminating heretics but by affirming the experience of the communion of saints. The church took and still takes the risk of recognizing the saints.

3. Another asset of the Orthodox is freedom from conditioned thinking and set theological "systems". Religious confessions destroy each other in theological disputes and even in religious wars because of self-righteousness and closed systems. The Orthodox have a rich tradition of intermediate formulas of multiple significance. This legacy can be extremely relevant today when people are afraid that unity may merely mean passing from one confession to another.

4. There is an eschatology possible here and now, an end that is constantly possible, which breaks continuity and cannot be appropriated by either history or eschatology. Each individual Christian has received the charism of the Spirit, a gift of the coming kingdom.

NOTES

[1] Cf. Emilianos Timiadis, *The Nicene Creed: Our Common Faith* (Philadelphia: Fortress, 1983), pp.93f.

[2] W.A. Vissser 't Hooft, "The Super-Church and the Ecumenical Movement," *Ecumenical Review*, X, 4 (July 1958), 365-85; cf. Philip Potter's remarks in his report to the Vancouver assembly (1983): "The calling of the churches to be a fellowship of confessing, of learning, of participation, of sharing, of healing, of reconciliation, of unity and expectancy has precisely been the preoccupation and task of the World Council. What consequences does this reality pose for the churches and for the Council? Can the churches go on behaving as though the Council belongs to their external rather than their internal relations? Can the Council allow itself, through the decision of representatives of the churches, to go its own way with programmes and activities reaching to groups and others, but not conceived, planned, communicated at all stages, and carried out with the active involvement of the churches?" (*Gathered for Life*, pp.208f.).

[3] Cf. Ion Bria, "The Eastern Orthodox in the Ecumenical Movement," *Ecumenical Review*, 38, 2 (April 1986), 226f.

[4] Cf. N.A. Nissiotis, "The Importance of the Faith and Order Commission for Restoring Ecclesial Fellowship," in *Sharing in Hope* (Geneva: WCC, 1979), p.16.

[5] *Jesus Christ — the Life of the World*, pp.9f.

IX. What Have the Orthodox Gained from the Ecumenical Movement?

What do they need from it?

The World Council of Churches looks to the ecumenical cause — unity — from the perspective of the renewal of the church, the human community and the world. *Renewal* has figured in many ecumenical discussions; for example, all the subjects in the WCC's fourth assembly (Uppsala 1968) were treated under this general heading. This emphasis is important because of its potential for bringing the churches of the Reformation and Orthodoxy into a fruitful dialogue on the question of *continuity* and *renewal*.[1] Recent discussions underline the New Testament view of the historical process as involving a series of "crisis" moments in which God's presence and action are forcefully revealed anew.[2] The dynamic of renewal includes sorting out or discerning the heritage by accepting the crisis, in the sense of bringing new aspects to light and changing by grace.

Renewal, of course, poses challenges and risks when it is perceived as a *structural* change. Every major WCC conference and assembly has spoken of the need to renew the structures of the "institutional life of the church". Nevertheless, the accent on renewal as the work of the Holy Spirit should be recognized as a major contribution of the WCC to the interpretation of church history. Orthodoxy will say that it is also theologically correct to take more seriously the renewal of creation, which is the work of the Holy Spirit and is prior to all renewal at the personal and community level.

On this point the WCC poses a very constructive challenge to the Orthodox: to look beyond themselves to the needs of the world, to emphasize the relation between God's people and God's world, to search for the points where the agenda of the people of God and the world's agenda intersect, to draw attention to the real problems of humanity which the church must take on to its agenda locally and universally. An important service of the Council is bringing into the local context the implications of the world situation. The local community must be concerned about what is happening elsewhere in the world. Catholicity is manifested in solidarity: each community standing for the whole.

Concern with the world's agenda does not mean activistic political expansion of the church; rather, it is an essential part of the church's mission into the world. Under the constraining power of God's love for humankind, under the imperative to call people to conversion and reconciliation, the Christian community becomes a sensitive community, struggling for a new kind of inner relationship and social life.

For the Orthodox, social and economic commitments to the renewal of the human community are rooted in and related to "the bread of life". "Christians who have heard the word and received the bread of life should henceforth be living prophetic signs of the coming kingdom."[3] It is critical to underline this aspect of Christian community and explore theologically the idea of the church as "sign":

> The church is called to be a prophetic "sign", a prophetic community through which and by which the transformation of the world can take place. It is only a church which goes out from its eucharistic centre, strengthened by word and sacrament and thus strengthened in its own identity, resolved to become what it is, that can take the world on to its agenda. There never will be a time when the world, with all its political, social and economic issues, ceases to be the agenda of the church. At the same time, the church can go out to the edges of society, not fearful of being distorted or confused by the world's agenda, but confident and capable of recognizing that God is already there.[4]

To be sure, there are many risks in assuming a prophetic role. How to assess the world situation remains a stumbling block. It may be difficult to provide an adequate theological basis for the options taken. The urgency of a situation may evoke quick action with all the accompanying chance of error. The WCC is under constant criticism for the options it does take. Of course, the Council must liberate itself from the temptation to defend its decisions and actions in ideological terms.

Membership of the WCC has taught the Orthodox a great deal about the organic association between the search for visible unity and the struggle for human liberation, justice and life. These are complementary demands of the gospel. New elements in the understanding of unity bring new energy to the search for an order of justice and peace, and vice versa. In fact, many of the controversial international issues raised by the Council stem from contextual difficulties in the life and mission of the member churches and thus interact with the problem of unity.

Christians at large should be more aware of how far the ecumenical ethos has inspired and determined human and political relationships among peoples and nations in certain areas. A break in ecumenical unity would undoubtedly undermine many efforts to achieve human reconciliation and peace today.

The Council has also provided a framework for discussing the reception of the confession of the apostolic faith in contemporary terms. The proliferation of consensus statements on particular theological and ethical issues cannot be ignored. How fundamental are such statements in relation to the common confession of faith? Both ecumenical discussions and bilateral dialogues confront the churches with the same problem: a new formulation of the creed, which is the apostolic faith in contemporary terms.

Many churches consider it too early to experiment with a "new creed" since they cannot fully assess what its implications would be. Actual reception of the apostolic faith could be a realistic ecumenical endeavour if it were accompanied by a sense of theological development and by an experience of ecclesial renewal in all churches. Therefore, the way in which the unity of faith is proposed as a major forthcoming project of the ecumenical movement demands careful attention. This must not merely be a confirmation of what preceded or of what the churches possessed in the past, but rather a movement towards a concrete discovery, or rediscovery, of the truth of Christ as the common source of life.

The WCC has provided a solid framework within which the churches have been able to clarify and redefine the essential terms and conditions of their ecumenical engagement. Orthodox theological development has been promoted and facilitated through ecumenical dialogue and encounter. Yet the themes of ecumenical theological research remain too confined within the framework of the Reformation. Although the terms of the discussion have become more catholic, treating wider issues of ecclesiology and soteriology, they are still unable to break free from these "systems". Often the proposals made by the Orthodox are not understood by those in Western churches, and Western proposals attract little attention from the Orthodox. Nevertheless, the response — even to ancient controversies — no longer automatically takes the form of polemic reaction.

The Orthodox have repeatedly called for more specificity in the debates on the unity of faith and on the content of this faith. This has given many the impression that the Orthodox perception of unity overemphasizes the doctrinal content of faith at the expense of on putting it into action. It has also been said that there is a difficulty in grasping what the Orthodox mean by "mystical" theology. The words of the patristic period have lost their meaning today. Moreover, Christians can talk about the same faith and mean different things, as evidenced by the way they live.

A synthesis of spiritualities

Exploring the great variety of styles in evangelism has led the Council to a deeper understanding of the eucharist as a missionary event and recognition of a liturgically oriented mission as part of the mainstream of the missionary movement. Orthodox have high hopes for this integration. They ask that more attention be given to how both liturgy and proclamation can take place in the present world situation. In many situations, the liturgy is no longer the ceremonial feast of an institutional body at the centre of society, but an existential experience at the margins of society. There is a great need to widen the horizon of evangelism and to gain a fresh understanding of the nature of mission itself within the context of celebration and worship. The Orthodox prefer to speak of *evangelizing communities*, whose life centre is the eucharist.

The issue of gospel and culture — of various cultural expressions of the Christian faith and diverse forms of Christianity — has also come into focus. This implies not only a theological openness in order to understand the role of secular and religious ideologies in the formation of contemporary culture, but also a deep sensitivity to people of other faiths and ideologies.

"Ecumenical spirituality" is a great benefit for the Eastern churches, enabling them to learn from the experiences of others in different situations. Different cultural and confessional backgrounds often build up barriers to spontaneous mutual correction and sustenance; and ecumenical interaction helps them to discover their own spirituality by seeing their own situation from another perspective.

The Orthodox have also discovered in the ecumenical community a witnessing awareness, a spirit of sharing faith, a recognition of others and of the church for others. These experiences have been tremendously enriching for the Orthodox in terms of the personal, existential commitment of Christians to the wider fellowship of the community. The sense of belonging to the community and the concept of edification of the body have perhaps diminished the experience of existential participation and of personal conversion of believers in Orthodox spirituality.

The practice among Christians of mutual continued intercession for one another is of great value, because it keeps before every Christian something of the catholicity of the church of Christ. It enables the churches to see one another, not with the eyes of confessional appraisal and historical assessment, but as joint petitioners before the throne of God. Intercession helps us to see what we *need* from other churches, opening us not only to giving but also to receiving within a fellowship of prayer and service.

Preserving its integrity does not require the Orthodox church to see itself as a monolithic confessional body that does not need the prayers and solidarity of the ecumenical fellowship. The ecumenical identity of Orthodoxy must not be seen as a counter-identity ("non-Protestant"). The existence of other Christians and churches is not a threat for the Orthodox. The Orthodox must recognize the distinct realities and signs of the Holy Spirit in the life and mission of other confessions. Moreover, the church cannot separate what God has put together: unity in the communion of the church and the renewal of human community.

Some Orthodox have been vocal critics of the ecumenical prominence accorded to the world's agenda and especially to local and global political conflicts. They claim that ecumenical issues are suffocated by political questions. But Orthodox people do recognize that *ecumenism of solidarity* with the poor and oppressed constitutes an important dimension of the search for visible unity in our times. Unity is not a private affair. There is a strong interconnection between *communion* and *solidarity*. The church is in danger of becoming "a world apart", not only within its own membership (with male-female and clergy-lay discriminations), but also for the human community at large (with its rich-poor, North-South, black-white and other conflicts). The first is an internal ecclesiological crisis. Through the Ecumenical Decade of Churches in Solidarity with Women, the Council is trying to heal this crisis. The second involves crises in society, politics and economics, brought to prominence by the WCC's Justice, Peace and Integrity of Creation (JPIC) emphasis. Both the Decade and JPIC are rooted in a profound commitment to the "conciliar process", which the Orthodox should support as an important development of ecumenical convictions and attitudes at the end of this millennium.

Responding to the Nairobi Assembly (1975) report on *Confessing Christ Today*, some Eastern churches raised notes of caution about the discussion of common witness. There is a constant demand from the Orthodox side to work primarily at the level of seeking a common expression of the doctrine of faith, of increasing awareness of doctrinal concerns and of recognizing the ecclesiological limits to common witness. These reactions are a reminder that the notions of common witness and common action should not be welcomed so enthusiastically that they come to be taken as a substitute for visible unity. The Orthodox are wary of any expression or manifestation of unity which is not rooted in and related to eucharistic communion, the cornerstone of ecumenical life.

Different views on unity are implied in the experience of common witness. Common witness both generates unity and makes visible the true nature of divisions. It often anticipates doctrinal agreement, as was suggested at the World Conference on Mission and Evangelism in Melbourne (1981). There are of course practical and doctrinal limitations to common witness. But there are several indications today that common Christian witness is a promising and creative reality in many local churches, communities and groups within the ecumenical fellowship. Increasingly, the ecumenical situation throughout the universal church is determined by the experience of joint action in a wide spectrum of activities: mission, evangelization, diakonia, inter-church aid, human rights struggles, Bible translation, theological education, catechetical work, dialogue with people of other faiths, common prayer and intercession.

Common Witness, a 1981 study document of the Joint Working Group between the Roman Catholic Church and the World Council of Churches, reflects the emergence of this practice. Even if common Christian witness cannot replace theological debate in the search for unity within a common faith, it can help Christians to give an immediate visibility and vitality to their incomplete universality, and to realize a vision of catholicity in the midst of the still existing historical separation. One could apply the same principle to the common eucharistic celebration.

Ecumenical participation is also helping the Orthodox to appreciate the distinctive confessional features of other churches. A constant temptation of ecumenical encounter is to compare different confessional traditions in an exclusive way, forgetting the legitimacy of diversity and the specificity of mission. In fact, the historical confessions bring substantial insights into ecumenical theology today. We may highlight three of the different ecclesiological emphases and approaches as follows:

1. There is an *institutional* approach to the church in Roman Catholic theology. This approach cannot merely be reduced to the question of the organizational structure of the church. The church is made up of people called to become the Body of Christ, a symbol of humanity and servant to all nations. The historic persistence of a visible Christian fellowship overcoming all barriers is part of the mission of the church and of the

doctrine of salvation. This view emphasizes, therefore, the institutional preoccupation and protection of the church. Mission is a response to a biblical mandate to incorporate everyone into the Body of Christ.

Does this appear to be a restrictive ecclesiology? If it insists on the "canonical limits" of the church, trying to restrict catholicity to the visible universality of Christendom, there *is* a tendency to see the ecumenical movement as an extension of the universality of Christendom, or even as a reconstruction of the *Pax Romana*. Catholics have not been very successful in avoiding this incoherence. Recent debate has in fact been reduced to mutual recognition of the *ecclesiality* of the Christian churches on the basis of valid sacraments of baptism, eucharist and ministry. Even the ecclesiology of communion, which remains a positive development in current ecclesiological dialogue, projects the view of an exclusive universality.

2. The Protestant tradition has adopted a *critical* theology which views everything in the life of the church as both historical and eschatological. Within this theological framework we can understand the relation between the nature of the church and the destiny of humankind. This view of *oikoumene* is grounded in the affirmation that Jesus Christ is both the Lord of all creation and the life given to all creation (cf. Colossians 1:18-20). The church signifies not only the ecclesial institution, the visible community of God's people in history, but also the dynamic movement of God towards humanity and all creation, which summons people of all nations and of all ages to become a pilgrim people. Commitment to the service of humankind springs from a view of humanity and the whole of creation as already having been visited and assumed by the power of the kingdom.

Ecclesiology is therefore not merely a doctrine of the church as institution with a dogmatic structure and canonical order. It also includes a worldview which locates humanity (both individuals and society) within God's purpose. By its nature, the community of God's people, living in history, is a distinct pilgrim people existing within the larger human pilgrimage. In this common pilgrimage Jesus Christ gives new life and new reality to the human community. Only then can it meet the most profound human needs in any concrete situation.

3. Orthodox theology has underlined the principle of *communio*, which is an echo of the link Orthodoxy makes between the *koinonia* of the Holy Trinity and ecclesial life. The trinitarian understanding of God is the basis for Christian life. Therefore, Orthodox cannot understand *personal* faith outside the faith of *community*. The essence of God's economy of

salvation is the life that streams forth from the source of the all-life-giving Trinity and proceeds into, and now abides with, all things.

Eastern theology believes in a unity which springs from the heart, mind and purpose of God. The unity sought is a unity within God, which God possesses in himself and offers to us in his Son. God is unity; and in the incarnation, cross and resurrection of Jesus Christ there is unity with him. This is a unity of a special nature, sacramental in essence, which is experienced by the disciples and the apostolic community, by all members of the church, when — and to the extent that — it is shared with the world. It is one organic process involving humanity and creation as a whole rather than individuals for their own sake.

The Orthodox also closely link the universality of the church with the image of Christ as *Pantokrator*, the one who brings eschatology and glorification — *basileia* — into history. Christ as *Pantokrator* has absolute rule over all creation, bringing under his own power all things, which mysteriously show forth his brightness and majesty. The risen Christ, the glorious Kyrios, Love itself unites and binds together all things in a mutual communion. Orthodox paintings of the resurrection make vivid this loving movement of the risen Lord. Seated on the celestial throne, he draws all things to himself. The Orthodox understanding of the sacredness of creation and the universality of love draws on this wide vision of Christ-*Pantokrator*.

At the heart of Orthodox preaching of the gospel of Jesus Christ is a deep understanding and experience of the resurrection. This is not only because the biblical story of the passion and resurrection is at the heart of the New Testament, but also because the community experiencing the risen Christ is an incipient sign of *basileia*. An excellent summary of the feast of resurrection is found in a famous paschal homily of St John Chrysostom (d.407), which speaks of the kingdom being manifested here and now in the risen Lord. The economy of salvation is now accomplished, the Lord joyfully invites all to share in his victory. Forgiveness springs from the tomb, death has lost its force, life gains eternity. There is no sin that exceeds God's abundant grace, there is no death that limits the *Pantokrator*'s life. Fear of death, despair and depression are all overcome by the abundance of life. This is what the resurrection means.

*   *   *

Ecclesiology has been a much controverted subject in ecumenical discussions. It is widely agreed that past ecclesiologies have made it difficult for Christians to understand not only such internal issues as the relationship between state and church or the role of lay people but also the wider ecumenical community. To put the point sharply, the critical problem is the very relevance of ecclesiology itself.

Ecclesiology should help people to understand anew the meaning of religion, humanity, salvation, culture and values, issues on which the traditional language of the church has become largely irrelevant. We should build a conciliar church, a fellowship of the Holy Spirit. This will include both people who have died for their faith and thus contributed a deep sense of certainty and integrity to the body and those who experience no certainty, but bring openness and a sense of humility.

Old ecclesiology justified an old society, but it provides little of spiritual value for people living in today's society. The ideology of solidarity failed, the gospel and culture dialogue was ignored. In the past, the relationship between church and state left much to be desired.

The paradoxical character of the church should be recognized, and its inability adequately to embody its experience should be acknowledged.

NOTES

[1] Cf. *Uppsala 68 Speaks* (Geneva: WCC, 1968), p.16: "The Holy Spirit has not only preserved the church in continuity with her past; he is also continuously present in the church, effecting her inward renewal and re-creation... The church is faced by the twin demands of continuity in the one Holy Spirit and of renewal in response to the call of the Spirit amid the changes of human history".

[2] Thomas Wieser, ed., *Whither Ecumenism?* (Geneva: WCC, 1986), pp.37-39, 99-101.

[3] *Orthodox Thought*, p.37.

[4] *Gathered for Life*, p.50.

X. Inter-Orthodox Unity

Every local church has its ecumenical witness in a given place as a member of national or regional councils. At the global level, Orthodoxy tries to formulate common positions and take common actions. The third preconciliar conference (Chambésy, 1986) adopted a document on *Orthodoxy and the Ecumenical Movement* which expressed a common point of view.[1] Without analyzing this text in detail, we should raise the following questions: Is inter-Orthodox unity an active basis for sustaining ecumenical development? To what extent can the Eastern churches say that this unity (or lack of unity) has a positive (or negative) effect in promoting local or global ecumenism? What are the most urgent issues faced by the Orthodox in relation to their inner conciliar life and their ecumenical participation?

Redefinitions

First of all, there are difficulties in interpreting the ecumenical agenda and in communicating with others. Individual churches have sometimes formulated positions on ecumenical issues or provided guidelines for their delegates to ecumenical meetings.

The preparatory work for the Great Synod has made it obvious that the understanding of ecumenism remains potentially divisive among Orthodox theologians themselves. The most influential group compares and evaluates the two epochs of the history of the church — the perfect unity of faith and spirituality prior to the separation of the eleventh century and the divided Christian world of the present — and concludes that there should be a moratorium of ecumenical dialogue because an inadequate methodology is being applied.

This interpretation is exaggerated by those who consider the history of the ecumenical councils as the only history of the undivided church and portray the early unity of faith over against later heretical formulations. For them, the church was divided by theological differences. Any reunion implies re-examination of these inherited theological issues and a return to the earlier period of unity. The ecumenical council, the institutional organ of the universal church, is the supreme authority to proclaim reunion of divided Christians.

As a matter of fact, the Oriental (non-Chalcedonian) churches state clearly that it is they who have maintained unity and orthodoxy of faith. Without formal reception of the Council of Chalcedon, they preserved Orthodox Christology in their own creeds because there was a common understanding and reception of the tradition outside the canonical synodical system, which operated primarily and most successfully in the framework of the Byzantine world.

The preparatory work for the Great Synod, which is an instrument to reinforce inter-Orthodox unity, has shown that actualizing this conciliar practice reveals new problems. For example, there is the decline of traditional "Christendom", especially of such historical centres of regional unity as Constantinople, Antioch, Alexandria, Jerusalem, Moscow. The so-called "imperial churches" have lost much of their influence abroad, having found it difficult to cope with the "universality" of the church; and their internal problems are serious. Other local churches sometimes play important conciliar roles. At the same time, Orthodoxy as a whole is enriched by the emergence of new churches in the diaspora — in Europe, Africa, Latin America and Asia — which no longer depend on their mother churches, having become "sister" rather than "daughter" churches.

The most significant change over the last few decades has been the redefinition by local churches of their identity, mission and service. There are many reasons for this: the appearance of new missionary situations created by secularization and militant evangelistic campaigns, the need to sanctify the life of the nation, which was compromised by political powers, and new possibilities for common Christian witness. Ecumenical perspectives cannot be separated from the difficult task of self-understanding and rediscovery of the calling of the people of God in a given time and place.

Ecumenical solidarity is needed to meet such challenges. Often, however, international movements and networks, out of a kind of naive universalism, prevent local churches from discovering their own potential for renewal and ecumenical life in their own situations.

No single theology or culture can claim to be the *centre* of Orthodoxy. Already after the apostolic period, difficulties arose in relating the gospel tradition to the new community born at Pentecost. How could the church theologically interpret this community as the new people of God, constituted in Christ, and in which there was neither discrimination nor disunity?

The church faced theological challenges from certain heresies which sought to rescue the Jewish monotheistic tradition, to bind the gospel of Jesus Christ to the New Testament writings and to reduce the history of salvation to the church. At the same time, it faced the historical temptation of binding the gospel to the history and geography of the Roman Empire. Concentration on the doctrinal controversy during the period of the ecumenical councils thus constituted a turning point in church history. The church was forced to recover the original tradition of the gospel as salvation and unity for all. It avoided giving the New Testament either a nationalistic or a universalistic dimension (as the religion of the Roman Empire). This was, therefore, a moment both of reassertion of cosmic Christology and of ecumenical awareness of the church.

However, the temptation to become a "Byzantine" imperial Christianity re-appeared at different times and in different forms. At the time of the Reformation, the Orthodox faced the old temptations in a new guise: either to remain a Byzantine, Eastern Christianity, complete with its national values and traditions, or to become one of the new confessional bodies.

The Greek-Byzantine patristic tradition grew and expanded while the Eastern church was limited to the Byzantine sphere. This tradition was carried to different areas by many people. But even though the majority of Orthodox churches today exist outside the areas of Byzantine culture, there is still a tendency, even in inter-Orthodox conferences, to invoke the Byzantine tradition as a common theological reference. The Byzantine legacy does provide a common theological frame of reference for Eastern Christianity as a whole, but it cannot substitute for and must not inhibit reception of theological contributions expressing the experience of the various local churches.

The multitude of voices within the contemporary Orthodox family and the great variety of their witness reflects a diversity of cultures and pastoral commitments. The recomposition of global unity must take account of all situations, possibilities and styles of witness. Polyphony becomes a necessary principle: recognizing the other who speaks a different language, is of different nationality, lives in a different cultural milieu, comes from a different social context.

The image of the next Great Synod will be different, because the image of the Orthodox *pleroma* is different. Recent pan-Orthodox debate on the emerging local churches in *diaspora* has made it obvious just how difficult it is to describe the image of the Orthodox *pleroma*. Again, the tension between fidelity towards the Holy Tradition and the continuity of ecclesiastical institutions which claim a pan-Orthodox validity is important. Also, the traditional structure of the *pleroma* has turned out to be more important and vital than the alternative structures necessitated by the actual configuration of the diaspora, with its urgent pastoral needs.

A deeper comprehension of holiness, repentance and sin in the institutional life of the church is needed. The view that the objective holiness of the church cannot be spoiled by the sin of Christians[2] fails to take account of ambiguities in the life of the church — the sinful duality of human history. Emerging from an idealistic interpretation of the history of Christendom, without reference to the church as a sociological community, this view is opposed by those who believe that the churches' recent experiences under oppressive political structures and destructive ideologies were the consequence of their failure to be a credible sign of the kingdom. Because of its weakness, the church closed its eyes to social sin.[3] Ecclesiastical authorities are accused of indifference to the precarious existence of many Christians, as well as to the plight of the weakest and poorest of the world, especially those whose suffering reaches the extreme of surrender to death. While the Orthodox pray, "Do not look to our sins, but to the faith of the church", they believe that the church cannot deny its implication in and responsibility for the recent history of suffering and division.

One of the most important challenges is thus to analyze critically the church's actions within history, rather than continuing to bypass controversial issues. The church must avoid the escapism of ignoring injustice, violence, human suffering and distress. Especially critical is "the witness of social justice in the name of the poor and the oppressed. We must re-learn the patristic lesson that the church is the mouth and voice of the poor and the oppressed in the presence of the powers that be. In our own way we must learn once again 'how to speak to the ear of the King' on the people's behalf."[4]

Without going into detail, we can say that the church, fascinated by the ancient tradition, the "return to the sources" and its own identity and continuity, has given the impression of being too timid to judge its own history. But keeping faithfulness and obedience together in historical continuity necessitates accepting new forms of Christian presence and mission that arise from historical crises.

What is positive and what is negative in the historical development of the church? A merely *canonical* transmission of the tradition prevents the church from answering this question. The church builds artificial bridges between traditional and contemporary times, between obedience to the gospel and the continuity of institutions, thus creating a discrepancy between symbol and reality, between the monumental traditional image of the church and its historical human face as a "people of God" who have gone through a liberating crisis. One of the weak points in contemporary theology is its failure to consider conceptually and pastorally the antagonistic elements within the society of the church.

Part of the Byzantine heritage was "the imperial idea of a universal Christian state", which guided the relations between state and church.[5] Especially in modern times, the state has had a nationalistic interest in defending the church. Today, local churches are less dependent on the intervention of their respective states. In many countries there was domestic opposition to the totalitarian state. Nationalistic conflicts among ethnic groups are resurfacing in a new and stronger way. All this calls the churches to rethink their historical alliances with political powers and find new ways to serve the people at large. This service is severely limited by the fact that social ethics and political action are still seen as part of an ecclesiology of the church-as-symbol which needs to be redefined.

There are situations which push the churches to intervene in public life, to denounce the abomination of the power of institutions and ideologies and to express their views regarding "political regimes". There is a risk here of teaching "social doctrines" or "playing politics", but it has been part of the democratic endeavour of the church in many countries to combat attacks on human dignity. How did pan-Orthodox solidarity function in the case of Serbian Orthodox priests and faithful when they were martyrs in their own country during the fascist occupation? Do we remember in our prayers the name of Bishop Gorazd of Prague, who paid with his life for taking part in the anti-fascist resistance in Czechoslovakia?

One must acknowledge that concerns for religious liberty, human rights, economic justice and human dignity have not been pressing items on the church agenda. There has been a terrible pressure for churches uncritically to legitimate the dominant policies of the state. The church must recognize that it is Christianly unacceptable to praise and sustain oppressive systems and confess that it has very often failed in protecting the victims under the cross.

Solidarity demands pastoral care for those marginalized or abandoned by a political regime, whether in one's own country or elsewhere. Social systems, with their monolithic ideologies and resort to violence, make the integration of different categories and classes of people difficult. As a result, dissident groups arise at the periphery of society, deprived of responsibility and experiencing non-commitment and frustration. They are unjustly cast out from society. The church should share abundantly its new experience of Christ, sometimes requiring costly obedience, but always a source of renewal and of new vision.

Eastern Christianity, with its historical heritage of national churches, isolated for centuries from wider Christian contacts and little interested in local ecumenism, is now moving into a period of renewal. It has a long and deep experience of endurance through difficulties.

Churches not in communion with the Orthodox

The Orthodox must also express themselves on an old and complex question: the ecclesial identity of other churches. In the light of the common identity as people of God, what are the actual ecclesial realities, provisional or incomplete though they may be, which can be recognized as signs and bonds of unity among the churches? What are the criteria for recognition and communion?

On the one hand, the Orthodox cannot ask that every aspect of the apostolic tradition should be reflected in the life of the church today. Even in the ancient churches, for example, there were different biblical canons, but they were not for that reason divided. On the other hand, the Orthodox cannot accept the dismissal of objectively divisive doctrinal issues as "confessional diversity". In past controversies, a formal judgement was sometimes passed on other churches, applying categories of schism and heresy that often seem inappropriate today. There is still a tendency to classify the churches too quickly into exclusive confessional categories. What is needed therefore is not only a new exploration into the confessional traditions, but also a new methodology that discerns between institutions which are permanent and those which are historically variable — between the irreconcilable positions and legitimate distinctive positions which are protected in the context of the WCC by the Toronto Declaration.

Ecclesiology seen from the pneumatological point of view is the key to such a methodology. One cannot speak of the church and its catholicity without reflecting on how the Holy Spirit relates to the various ecclesial realities and ecumenical experiences. Already in the 1950s, Georges Florovsky emphasized that the Orthodox recognize the existence of ecclesial realities and institutions outside the canonical limits of the church. There is, he said, an intermediary charismatic sphere. This is not a marginal or residual, but an area of diversity (even confessional diversity) that does not contradict the common identity.[6]

Today, the Orthodox are ready to recognize not only many signs of unity and specific vocations in different places or regions (signs and vocations which have a symbolic meaning for all — which are, in other words, "catholic"), but also sacramental signs and acts and apostolic continuity in many churches. The next step is to apply these criteria to the practice of eucharistic communion. A positive sign is that the Orthodox are now going beyond the general affirmation — eucharistic communion must be seen in the light of an ecclesiology of communion — to specify the concrete issues involved: the church's ministry and the sacramentality of ministry.

A pneumatological entry point would help in perceiving these ecclesial realities and ecumenical experiences outside the canonical limits of the Orthodox church. For example, there is a movement *(oikonomia)* of the Spirit in history which not only edifies and unites the Body of Christ, but also opens up new situations in which the grace of God may be revealed and received. This understanding of the universal presence and action of the Spirit is important for the ecumenical openness of the historic churches. Here, the Orthodox have a criterion for recognizing different ecclesial realities and responding to ecumenical situations, as well as a means of understanding differences outside the Orthodox church:

> Generally the Orthodox avoid giving precise definitions of the ecclesial status of non-Orthodox Christians and churches, not because they are indifferent to doctrinal matters but because they feel that the soteriological consequences of heresy and/or schism should be left to the judgement of God. They concentrate on maintaining the positive witness to the truth for which they feel responsible. The questions arising in the encounter with the non-Orthodox vary from church to church. As the Orthodox meet Protestants they must ask the question as to how the ontological unity and identity of the church can be expressed without a permanent and visible criterion of unity in the midst of infinite variations and even contradictions in creed and in church structure created by historical change.[7]

From the perspective of the Holy Spirit, the catholicity of the church is conceived in terms of the realization of the fullness of God's grace and of God's involvement in the wholeness of creation, rather than in terms of a totality of Christendom. In historical terms, the catholicity of the church demands a fuller and more organic integration of the Eastern and Western traditions. This is necessary, not simply for historical reasons — since all are products of one or both of these traditions — but also because there are serious dangers in each tradition which can only be avoided if there is integration and synthesis.[8]

Eastern and Oriental Orthodox together

In various places, Eastern churches and people are confronted with situations that require contextual responses, common witness and pastoral solutions. For example, while recognizing the difficulty of overcoming the theological differences and disputes from which Eastern and Oriental churches have suffered for centuries, we believe that through immediate common witness and mission around the world these churches will rediscover their full and visible unity.

We raise the issue of communion between Eastern and Oriental churches because there is an immediate possibility for such unity and because it indicates how Orthodox could be approached by other churches on the matter of eucharistic communion.[9]

It is a peculiar anomaly of the ecumenical scene that there is no sacramental/eucharistic communion between Eastern and Oriental Orthodox Churches. No formal excommunication separates them; therefore, neither can canonically deny the other. Yet due to historical accidents, they have remained in a status of non-communion. Living historically separate has not meant that they have lost their identity: both churches are faithful to the apostles and faithful to diverse rites as local churches living in various nations and cultures.

Throughout history, attempts to put an end to this division did not succeed for a variety of reasons. Nevertheless, many occasions were recorded when people — lay or clergy — did deal with each other with full conviction that both parties held the proper Orthodox belief in the person of our Lord.

In the last thirty years, several joint consultations of Eastern and Oriental Orthodox theologians have been organized (Aarhus 1964, Bristol 1967, Geneva 1970, Addis Ababa 1971). The Geneva conference in particular raised several issues which are at the heart of this unity.[10]

An official theological dialogue between the two church families began in 1985 in Chambésy. Since then, several official meetings have taken place, and these conversations confirmed what the non-official discussions discovered: both traditions share the same Orthodox doctrine of Christology.

The WCC, which accepts the churches' exclusive authority to decide on conditions of unity and on the form of their visible union, has followed the evolution of this dialogue with interest. Here is a particular example where historical factors can divide or unite the church.

Common convictions

In looking at the possibility of eucharistic communion and mutual recognition of sacraments between Eastern and Oriental Orthodox Churches, several facts should be kept in mind:

— Both traditions belonged to the undivided church before the Council of Chalcedon (451). The Nicene-Constantinopolitan Creed (325 and 381) remains the cornerstone of their unity.

— In neither church did the historical evolution of the Christological formulations alter the basic common affirmation of the person of the *Monogenis*. The text of the eucharistic liturgy of both traditions incorporates common Orthodox affirmations, for example, the *Monogenis*.

— The two church families agree doctrinally on both apostolic succession and sacraments, which are the most important elements in any discussion of eucharistic communion. Worship in both traditions is organized around the sacraments. The eucharistic liturgy has the same order and text.

— Each church has distinctive doctrinal accents and liturgical traditions, which should be seen as indispensable parts of the one Orthodoxy. The core of the doctrine of the seven ecumenical councils was preserved in both traditions in various ways. An agreement signed on 19 November 1987 in the Amba Bishoy monastery in Egypt by four Orthodox leaders of the Middle East (Patriarchs Shenouda III and Parthenios III of Alexandria, Ignatios IV of Antioch, and Catholicos Karekin II of Cilicia, with Syrian Patriarch Ignatios Zakka Ivas of Antioch also expressing his agreement) speaks of "the profound communion of faith which exists among the Eastern and Oriental Orthodox" (see Appendix II).

— Common liturgical elements and spiritual practices can easily be recognized in the two traditions. Both have the same *typicon* (order of service) and the same spirituality (prayer of Jesus). The liturgical language is identical and has been preserved in Greek and in the Coptic translation. Fasting has a special value in both traditions. Certain saints are commonly venerated.

Reciprocal recognition and communion

The sacramental, eucharistic communion between Eastern and Oriental churches is a matter of full reciprocal recognition, motivated by their unity of faith, explicitly or implicitly expressed, and required by the pastoral situation in which they live.

Both Oriental and Eastern churches reciprocally recognize each other's baptism because they share the same baptismal faith — the creed of the first and second ecumenical councils. To believe in the true God and the true Christ is the faith of the church, which each of the baptized must accept. Once baptism is recognized, refusal of communion is an anomaly. Christ receives at his table those who become his disciples through the confession of faith which is at the heart of the sacrament of baptism.

One cannot separate Christ from his church, the head from the body. Through the confession of the faith and reception of baptism, the disciple becomes a member of the church. Reconciliation with Christ means communion with his church. Those who recognize the church as the Body of Christ and are incorporated into it through baptism are ready to receive the communion.

This ecclesial membership is an essential. It means that each is a member of the local church, presided by the local bishops elected by the faithful.

All Orthodox see the eucharist as the centre of Christian life. Both Eastern and Oriental confess the eucharistic communion that sustains the real life of the community: "I am the vine, you are the branches. He who abides in me, and I in him, he it is that bears much fruit, for apart from me you can do nothing" (John 15:5). Both maintain that apart from the eucharist there is no substance to the Christian life. Only the eucharist gives a plenitude of grace to our existence as disciples of Christ, members of the church and penitent sinners looking for the kingdom of God. This is the belief of both churches.

The church does not automatically distribute the sacrament of the eucharist. It is necessary to be accepted by the church, personally and explicitly, in order to participate in the communion. Christ gave the apostles and their successors the ministry of forgiveness. "Receive the Holy Spirit. If you forgive the sins of any, they are forgiven; if you retain the sins of any, they are retained" (John 20:22-23). The priest who receives the faithful into the church through baptism, who receives the confession of sins and pronounces their absolution, opens or closes the door for communion.

The essentials of the eucharistic practice are the same for both churches:
— The work of the Holy Spirit in the transformation of the bread and wine into the Body and Blood of Jesus Christ is affirmed.
— Both the bread and the cup are for the *laos* — the people.
— Both express diversity in liturgical practice: the rite, the way to celebrate and to fast. St Athanasius of Alexandria did not celebrate the same rite as St John Chrysostom. Nicholas Cabasilas accepted the Roman rite, but criticized the absence of *epiklesis* in the Latin doctrine of transubstantiation.

"Economy" — *oikonomia* — is the permission given the bishops as part of their pastoral responsibility to provide sacraments as a way of salvation and missionary response in a particular context and condition. It does not imply a new canonical order, but is an attitude of openness towards members and non-members of the church in order to help them to live a Christian life. It contradicts both proselytism and the idea of abandoning one's membership in the mother/original church. Christ opens the way to sinners in various forms. "Economy" means to respond to this mission in Christ's way.

There is no dogmatic, ecclesiological or sacramental obstacle to eucharistic communion between Eastern and Oriental Orthodox Churches. The sacrament of the eucharist is the sacrament of the church. Until explicit agreement on recognition of the sacraments and eucharistic communion can be reached between the two churches, the respective authorities should instruct the priests to practice it in the framework of "economy".

Both churches pray in the liturgy, "Let us love one another so that we may with one mind confess Father, Son and Holy Spirit, the Trinity one in essence and undivided." Love is the precondition for faith and not vice versa. The establishment of eucharistic communion by the Eastern and Oriental Orthodox is a matter of mutual love — that love "which is always ready to excuse, to trust, to hope and to endure whatever comes" (1 Corinthians 13:7).

NOTES

[1] *Episkepsis*, no. 369 (Dec. 1986), pp.14-17.
[2] "Declaration of the Eastern Orthodox Delegates Concerning the Main Theme of the [Second] Assembly," *Ecumenical Review*, VII, 1 (Jan. 1954), 67-69.
[3] Antoine Kartachoff has written, "It is high time we gave up using the divine nature of the church to cover up the sins and defects in church life, when the time comes to reform them

and make certain innovations... The church has a kernel of infallibility and a foundation which is impeccable, but certain aspects of it are subject to sin. The historic church... must have the courage to recognize its sins in history, its human weaknesses, the errors in its life and work, and must make an effort to correct them"; "Orthodox Theology and the Ecumenical Movement," *Ecumenical Review*, VIII, 1 (Jan. 1955), 33.

[4] Geevarghese Mar Ostathios, *The Sin of Being Rich in a Poor World* (Madras: CLS, 1983); cf. A. Papaderos, "Our Ecumenical Diakonia," in Slack, ed., *Hope in the Desert*, pp.91-106.

[5] John Meyendorff, *The Byzantine Legacy in the Orthodox Church* (Crestwood NY: St. Vladimir's, 1982), p.143.

[6] "The Doctrine of the Church and the Ecumenical Problem," *Ecumenical Review*, XI, 2 (April 1950), 158f.

[7] *Orthodox Contributions to Nairobi*, p. 12.

[8] Cf. John Zizioulas, "Eschatology and History," in Wieser, ed., *Whither Ecumenism?*, pp.70f.

[9] Cf. *Orthodox Contributions to Nairobi*, p.33.

[10] Paulos Gregorios, Wm. H. Lazareth and Nikos Nissiotis, eds., *Does Chalcedon Divide or Unite?* (Geneva: WCC, 1981).

XI. Crisis and Hope

In the ecumenical encounter the Orthodox churches have been able to share with others a wealth of theological ideas and nuances. A partial list of these, many of which we have touched on in preceding chapters, would include "reception", sacramental spirituality, ecclesiology of communion, the Trinity as a pattern of *koinonia*, recovering confidence in worship, the Christological centre and trinitarian source of our faith, the "liturgy after the liturgy", "eucharistic vision", the church as "mystery", the "catholic" significance of the local church, conciliar fellowship, mission as *martyria*, and *theosis* — growing more and more into God's likeness.

The Orthodox have been accustomed to identify the fundamental difference between the Eastern and the Western traditions as ecclesiological. Sometimes this involves an overestimation of a deductive ecclesiology. In recent years there has been a marked revival of interest in ecclesiology among churches or communities which have not traditionally shown much interest in this area — for example, a "Salvationist" or a "congregationalist" ecclesiology. Are these positive nuances, or will they only aggravate the confrontation in the ecumenical movement?

At the same time, the churches need profound wisdom when they lend their spiritual and moral voice to discussions in the arena of political decision-making. There should be less triumphalism in analyzing power structures and more radicalism in demystifying social and political systems. Any theology, whether "academic" or "liberation", runs the risk of becoming a false ideology about the people of God when facing the confusion and ambiguity of human history.

Furthermore, mission in an unbelieving world, in a society which is no longer a *corpus* of Christians, is a matter of renewal and spirituality, of practising the "priesthood" of all the people of God. The Orthodox continue to reinforce the value of "holiness", of the testimony of a Christlike life, in commending and enacting the gospel. One hopes that the old — and incorrect — distinction between "more missionary" and "less missionary" (or "non-missionary") churches will disappear from the ecumenical vocabulary.

Ecumenism is a decisive issue for the future of the church. The crisis of the conciliar process is not only that we do not know how to correlate questions of faith with social questions, but also that we are not able to confront new boundaries and sources of division with a vision of unity.

There is a complacency with the "cult of difference". "Tensions", "pluralities", and "conflictual distinctions" are dogmatized as a condition of ecumenical life, perceived as unfortunate but inevitable. This makes our vision insufficiently ecumenical. We should say openly that we seek not to be different in an antagonistic way, but to be faithful. And faithfulness to the gospel implies faithfulness to the fullness of gospel and to the richness of all traditions. Sometimes we use our imagination to be so radically different that we can no longer discern our unity (an example is the terminology used to confess our faith in the Triune God). Often we uncritically accept ambiguous principles in the interest of a plurality of traditions and theologies.

There is also a sense that we are not convinced about a common objective or frame of reference for ecumenical fellowship. In building our own traditions, we may lose sight of the tradition of reference which governs all Christian history. The new contextual interpretations may be inspired and accessible, but they should also maintain a transparency through which the original tradition may shine. Of course, tradition is not a museum.

A consultation about the plurality of cultures as part of the ecumenical fellowship, held in Cartigny in 1985, recognized that all churches, historical or independent, are displaced from an ecumenical setting for confessional and cultural reasons, because they have their own *tradition* (not biblical interpretations) about the incarnation and about the church. Everyone must move across lines of doctrine, culture and nationality in order to enter the framework of the larger ecumenical order. But nobody is taking concrete steps. In spite of its new "vision of ecumenism", the Roman Catholic Church is not ready to make the ecclesiological concessions necessary for this re-adaptation. The Reformation churches demonstrate that they alone cannot lead an ecumenical movement of universal scope. The Orthodox give signs of reluctance concerning unity as a conciliar fellowship. What powerful force might lead the churches to take their place inside the framework?

The pace of the conciliar process at the global institutional level is frustrating. Except for a few pathetically tentative steps, we are not very active in taking concrete initiatives towards unity. How long will this gradual approach to unity postpone the moment of eucharistic communion? Meanwhile, people at the grassroots are expecting this from ecclesiastical institutions. The real ferment of ecumenism comes out of the grassroots, but do we recognize completely the signs and fruits of unity when they are present? The more rich and varied is the local, contextual experience, the more time will be needed to grasp its ecumenical dimension. How many more generations will be required for ecumenism?

The last decade of this millennium is a fitting time to concentrate more on ecumenism in a positive sense. Often, the WCC has described ecumenism largely in negative terms. It is *not* an attempt to build a "super-church"; it is *not* aimed at changing the confessional affiliations of the member churches; it is *not* an invitation to be disloyal to one's tradition or to revise one's creeds.

The World Council of Churches is bound by basic membership agreements and will thus always have such proscriptions and interdictions. This original emphasis on a *protective* ecumenism provided an encouraging environment in which churches could emphasize their heritage. It promised a way to solve the problem of unity while retaining differences pertaining to each particular church. It also led to the formation of parallel small groups and alternative movements to satisfy the desire for unity outside formal institutional churches and to demonstrate signs of unity without challenging the essentials of the faith.

Later, a holistic approach to ecumenism has given the impression that the vision of unity is so vast and all-embracing that it has no definable limits. Calls for solidarity, common witness and open communion have indeed moved the churches from their traditional isolation, but they have neglected their essential internal problems, so that ecumenism has become an external affair.

The concept of unity has been distorted both by restrictive attitudes towards an inclusive, universal vision and by large public celebrations of the mass and big ecumenical gatherings, which responded to a sociological need in the 1980s. The paradox is that the churches are still sleeping under the shadow of their traditional confessionalism and nationalism and need a clear goal in order to reach ecumenical community. Part of the problem is that the ecumenical experiences generated by this reality are weak, unrelated and largely unknown. We need more description of concrete situations where ecumenical life is actually happening.

But the real issue is that we cannot go out of our own churches to practice ecumenism with empty minds and empty hands. That is dangerous, because it can lead to the loss of the little faith we have. If the kingdom is divided, if the struggle against any form of divorce is part of the unity, we have to carry forward the power of the faith that God himself will build his house. We do not steal the unity from him; we open our hearts and hands to his work of unity. The *a priori* of unity is the power of faith, which transforms us into the salt and light of the world.

The leaven of Christian koinonia

The founding of the WCC in 1948 was not the first occasion on which the Orthodox church showed itself open to ecumenical encounter and to removing obstacles on the path towards unity. The relations of the Orthodox with sixteenth-century reformers, their response to the invitation to the First Vatican Council, their initiatives for bilateral dialogue, the Encyclical Letter of the Ecumenical Patriarchate of Constantinople in 1920, the decision to convoke a Great and Holy Synod are all evidences of the choice by the Orthodox to travel the road of ecumenical fellowship.

Historical factors have sometimes prevented effective implementation of this basic desire. But when their situation eased a little, especially after World War II, the Orthodox family began to demonstrate its active ecumenical presence. Only recently has it rediscovered the extraordinary ecumenical work of several brilliant theologians and bishops from Orthodox churches in the Balkans and central Europe prior to the foundation of the WCC.

But if the role of the local Orthodox churches within the contemporary inter-confessional context attests to their importance and responsibility in the wider ecumenical effort, it must be said that the Orthodox church's entry into the ecumenical movement and the task of maintaining its presence there have not been easy. Right from the beginning, the Orthodox have insisted that their participation in the WCC is not as just one of the many confessional families, but as a bearer of the undivided church and thus offering a unique witness. Firmly convinced that their church is not a confessional form of Christianity, the Orthodox have refused to be limited by historical division. Therefore, the role of the Orthodox church should not be seen as one of passive testimony, but rather as one of active witness.

As a partner in common reflection, the Orthodox have come to understand the vast diversity and complexity of the ecumenical fellowship. They have discovered Christians and communities who, in spite of their separation (whether due to confessional, social or cultural factors), are deeply committed to the search for unity. Various ecclesiologies co-exist with various levels and forms of ecclesial practice; new possibilities for unity alternate with events that obscure or discourage the search for unity. This experience obliges one to acknowledge not only that "there has been no fundamental alteration in the ecumenical and ecclesiological principles of Orthodox teaching throughout this present era",[1] but also that, to a large extent, the major problems, concerns and expectations of the ecumenical community of today are part of the life of Orthodoxy itself.

Moreover, the presence of the Orthodox church in the WCC has not only prevented the Council from simply becoming a pan-Protestant federation, but has had an impact on its life and theological development. Orthodoxy has exhibited a dimension of theological problematics that goes beyond the Western churches' polarization between pre- and post-Reformation. Moreover, it has created a real *ecumenical* situation, representing a very large number of popular churches, within which the Council is called to act responsibly.

Ecumenical experience has encouraged a struggle for growth in integrity and wholeness. The prominence accorded to human and political issues around which conciliar fellowship is constituted represents a great accomplishment. But has this come at the price of being insensitive and inhospitable to the local churches? Who is questioning the changes taking place? The proliferation of very individual theologies, ecclesiologies and ecumenisms and the appearance of very culturally (if not ideologically) conditioned paraphrases of the Bible give the impression that the ecumenical movement sometimes extends diversity to include "matters of faith" and does not distinguish differences in priorities from conflicting priorities. What is needed is serious regulation of the various perspectives and emphases the churches promote and defend in serving the common ecumenical cause.

No confessional or cultural group possesses all the riches and insights of the *oikoumene*. Orthodoxy is not the *oikoumene*, but it bears a particular witness to the *faith of the church*, subject to the criteria of apostolicity and universality. The Orthodox have used a particular language to carry that tradition (verbal, doxological, visual), which guarantees a certain continuity, freedom and universality through space and time. Because it has such a base, it can give a testimony that Jesus' prayer "that all may be one" has an echo in the history of Christianity, unifying Christians in the multitude of spiritual and doctrinal divergences that exist. The Orthodox have encouraged the WCC to take seriously the theology of *koinonia* with God in order fully to live unity as a given reality both here and now and promised, and ecumenically to serve the renewal of the world.

There is no doubt that the Orthodox impact on the future of the ecumenical movement depends on their internal unity. The existence of the ecumenical movement itself obliges them to press forward in the service of unity. In the interest of a more authentic witness, they should renew the existing pan-Orthodox structures and institutions, and shape an Orthodox "symphony" in a new, contemporary and creative form. Thus the new generation of Orthodox looks forward to the pan-Orthodox Synod with great hope. Since the Orthodox claim to be the leaven in the universal, undivided church, they should also agree to stay in the mainstream of the ecumenical movement. Moreover, as the countries and societies where they live prepare for a new era of faith, they should assume the continuity of the apostolic church and search for new expressions of common witness and faith.

Where there is prayer for unity...

The churches have rediscovered the centrality of worship, the need for common celebration of faith, the ecumenical sense of the eucharistic liturgy, the extraordinary power of intercession for achieving convergence and building new relationships. The churches should maintain this inspiring vision, making visible the liturgical component of the ecumenical pilgrimage. *Lex orandi lex credendi* means churches and Christians, men and women, living by a faith embodied in a variety of theological and doxological affirmations.

Many churches and groups of Christians have confessional and missionary prayer cycles, litanies and liturgies according to their own traditions and calendars or based on concerns shared by local congregations. To a great number of people, this liturgical tradition is of central importance. But, as churches and Christians deepen their commitment to search together for full visible unity, there is another opportunity and need: a new spirituality of prayer and celebration is called for, which is the discovery not only of the profound God-given unity we hold in common, but also of the many concerns in which we differ. Intercessions for each other, singing hymns together, rejoicing in ecumenical prayer mean breaking down resistance and supporting each other in difficult situations.

Perhaps the most creative recent contribution of the ecumenical movement has been precisely in developing a vital sense of continued mutual intercession. Praying together as one family and appearing together before the world in response to the calling of Jesus Christ, Lord and Saviour, is an empowering and blessed sign of the communion of the saints. A real *metanoia* has happened in worship and celebration at ecumenical gatherings. The intention of unity is expressed in every prayer, since the name of our Lord, the Head of the Body, is named. There is an intention of catholicity and a power of *koinonia* in invoking the name of the Holy Spirit. The history of the church is full of saints, confessors and mystics who apprehended the divine mystery through prayer. Where there is no prayer for unity, there is no vision of unity.

Commemorations of the fortieth anniversary of the WCC frequently overlooked this area of *liturgical renewal* and *ecumenical spirituality*, including concern for mutual intercession and worship, prayer for unity and for renewal movements and groups. Too little was said about "spiritual ecumenism" as an important stream in the life of the churches during this period, although it has been one of the most dynamic resources of the ecumenical movement. It is the immediate task of the WCC to complete its "ecumenical memory" by affirming how the ecumenical cause is served by those committed to pray and worship together.

Christians believe that the power of prayer can change the life of an individual and renew the history of the church. All those who believe in church unity should pray together as one family. It is in joining together in prayer that the one body of Christ can make its common intercession "for the peace of the whole world, for the welfare of the holy churches of God, and for the union of all".

As we enter into a new period of ecumenical pilgrimage, let us invoke the Holy Spirit to give divine life and power to our human voices and cries for the unity of all God's people.

The Orthodox: central or isolated?

The Orthodox who were present at the WCC's seventh assembly (Canberra, Australia, 1991) drafted a separate statement — *Reflections of Orthodox Participants* — in which they expressed the difficulty they had in receiving the statements of the assembly, especially those related to the theology of the main theme: "Come, Holy Spirit — Renew the Whole Creation".[2] Two texts — one prepared by the delegation of the Ecumenical Patriarchate of Constantinople, the other by the Russian Orthodox

Church — sought to protect the integrity of Orthodoxy while at the same time saving the ecumenical movement, that is, "its goals and ideals, as formulated by its founders".

For the Orthodox churches, several tendencies and developments — departures from the Basis of the WCC, marginalization of concern for the restoration of the unity of the church, departures from biblically based Christian understanding, substitution of the spirit of the world for the Holy Spirit — have called into question the WCC's very nature and identity. Therefore they saw Canberra as a crucial moment in ecumenical history. In formulating their criticisms in a document which combined elements of the Russian Orthodox and Ecumenical Patriarchate drafts, the Orthodox emphasized that this is a matter of unity in faith and of fundamental Orthodox ecclesiology, not an expression of Orthodox triumphalism.

The "reflections" not only point to current tensions within the WCC, but also reveal the difficulty the Orthodox have in naming the specific challenges they wish to pose to the WCC *today*. On the one side, the WCC continues to argue, following the Reformation tradition, that there are tensions inherent in the ecumenical movement which cannot be overcome; on the other side, the Orthodox repeat the formulas of the 1950s and 1960s as the objective criteria for unity. Both give the impression that they are living in a different age of dialogue and cooperation.[3]

In what context should these "reflections" be seen? Some observers would see Canberra as manifesting that the WCC is a huge forum for theologies, spiritualities and political viewpoints which cannot be contained in a common framework. The assembly seemed to become, at many points, an emotional community which exaggerated this diversity, even creating the impression of syncretism. Considering that the WCC was giving priority to this unpredictable and uncontrolled element, the Orthodox had a sense of being encircled by liberal and sometimes offensive attitudes.

One of the serious questions in Canberra was concerning the Christian *oikoumene* itself. What about Christianity outside the WCC? Within the WCC the Orthodox feel isolated from their sister church, the Roman Catholic Church, which similarly underlines the structure of traditional Christianity. In what might be regarded as disengagement from the real problems and needs of today's world, the Orthodox gained the support of many who identified themselves as "evangelicals".

Ecumenism is still built on international relationships, rather than on ecumenical conversion at the local level. One of the major gaps at the Canberra assembly was the insufficient attention given to the building blocks of unity that have been realized in recent times. For example, the Eastern Orthodox spoke only timidly about the successful dialogue with the Oriental Orthodox. Instead, they emphasized a number of concerns "that have been developing among the Orthodox since the last assembly."

The perspective of eucharistic communion between the two Orthodox families, which illustrates the centrality of the restoration of unity to the ecumenical movement, was absent. Nor did they offer a critical view of their own situation or an objective vision of the present world. The Orthodox gave the impression of viewing the ecumenical movement with an outdated pessimism.

Orthodox ecumenical involvement requires serious analysis. The WCC needs greater awareness of the Orthodox contributions to the ecumenical movement, recognizing that many of these insights and principles are now shared widely among the churches in the WCC. The Orthodox must acknowledge that the understanding of ecumenism today implies the acceptance of these values. They themselves work for their implementation. But with minimum participation they cannot have maximum expectations.

The WCC's concern for other churches, communities and movements is not a matter of statistics. These communities have the same concerns and needs as the Orthodox: a need for transcendence and holiness, concerns for unity and diversity. They combine the spiritual and political expression of their experience. The WCC cannot suffocate this Christianity because of the fear of syncretism or compromise. It has to discern the meaning of their values for the whole ecumenical community. Their contributions must be brought into a perspective of unity inside the Council. The Orthodox should be aware, therefore, of the evolution of ecumenical ideas in the other parts of the *oikoumene*.

The WCC itself must analyze its own character and functions, not remaining rigidly fixed in its period of origin. There is one ecumenical movement, and the WCC is a faithful servant of that movement. It is clear that, beyond this Basis, the member churches perceive an ecclesial reality in the conciliar fellowship. The role of the Orthodox churches is not only to jog the memory of the WCC, but to help it to realize its nature in a positive sense.

Can we speak now about the ecclesial substance of the Council? As long as the Orthodox churches are not answering this question, they must learn to live with the dilemmas of the WCC.

Conclusion

Visible unity among churches implies not only a doctrinal knowledge of Christianity but also a living experience of Christ as common Lord and Head of the Body and of his Spirit, the Spirit of truth and communion. It is a process that requires both doctrinal and spiritual shifts, not because of any external pressure but out of obedience to him who prayed that "all may be one". His prayer is more than an affirmation or supplication: it is a firm warning that we exist only as the one people of God, which cannot be destroyed.

Orthodox can help to prepare the way for visible unity with an understanding of the full ecumenical community and of various forms of ecclesial life and order. But the Orthodox must renounce facile definitions and proscriptions. Jesus called the women and men he wanted (Mark 3:13), using them as he needed them, taking various initiatives and having the freedom to commit to diverse actions, recognizing them as part of the history of salvation.

We tend by contrast to keep the whole church to ourselves. We can stay together with many Christians because we have a common humanity, sharing the image of God. But our intimacy with God decreases and we lose our fervour and sense of communion with others (proscribed as "heterodox") when we view them in exclusive terms. Jesus needs all people, and therefore we must try to engage in dialogue with the whole ecumenical community, upon whom God bestows his continual blessings.

The Orthodox must re-examine the *a priori* of visible unity and weigh anew the burdens of the Tradition which are required as a condition for unity. We serve the truth by seeking the inner truth in various traditions, not by enslaving ourselves to doctrines which non-Orthodox are not ready to accept as part of their tradition.

There is room for diversity, for hearing what the Spirit is saying to the churches today. Recognition of others always involves a risk — but it is a risk which the Orthodox must take.

The Orthodox must realize that their role is not to guide Christians into the history of Christianity, but to remember that "each must order his life according to what the Lord has granted him" (1 Corinthians 7:11).

Unity is also an act of holiness, which means recognizing that the Christian community is vulnerable from every angle. The church has no certainty itself; it always depends on the Spirit and the faithfulness of the people. We must free ourselves from the idea that we produce unity out of human material and efforts. Conversations, intercessions and solidarity are necessary, but there comes a moment when all these stop and the Spirit takes over. We undermine our determination to advance towards unity if we are not able to confess that unity comes from above. In the kingdom of unity there is a room for repentance, the only way to make progress in holiness.

NOTES

[1] *Guidelines for Orthodox Christians in Ecumenical Relations* (New York: Standing Conference of Orthodox Bishops in America, 1973), p.50.

[2] Text in Michael Kinnamon, ed., *Signs of the Spirit* (Geneva: WCC, 1991), pp.279-282.

[3] Cf. David Gill, ed., *Gathered for Life* (Geneva: WCC, 1983), p.87: "A special consultation with official representatives of Eastern Orthodox churches was held in 1981. Several issues were discussed and have since been pursued, such as the inclusion of baptism in the Basis of the WCC, procedure and method of voting on matters of ecclesiological significance, and adequate Orthodox representation in the life of the Council. Further efforts should be made for strengthening relations with Orthodox member churches."

Appendixes

I. Roman Catholic - Eastern Orthodox Relations

This is the historic text lifting the mutual excommunications which created the schism of 1054. It was released on 7 December 1965, during the Second Vatican Council, by Pope Paul VI in Rome and the Ecumenical Patriarch Athenagoras I in Istanbul. The two had met in Jerusalem in January 1964.

1. Full of gratitude to God for the favour which is mercifully granted them in their brotherly meeting in those holy places where the mystery of our salvation was accomplished through the death and resurrection of the Lord Jesus, and where the church was born by the outpouring of the Holy Spirit, Pope Paul VI and Patriarch Athenagoras I have not lost sight of the intention which they held from then onwards, each for his part, never to omit in the future any of those gestures inspired by charity which might contribute towards the fraternal relations thus initiated between the Roman Catholic Church and the Orthodox Church of Constantinople. They believe that they are thus responding to the call of divine grace, which today requires that the Roman Catholic Church and the Orthodox Church, as well as all Christians, overcome their differences, so as to be once again "one" as the Lord Jesus asked of his Father for them.

2. Among the obstacles to be found in the way of the development of these brotherly relations of trust and esteem, there is the memory of those painful decisions, acts and incidents which led in 1054 to the sentence of excommunication delivered against Patriarch Michael Cerularius and two other persons by the legate of the Roman See led by Cardinal Humbertus, legates who were themselves in turn objects a similar sentence on the side of the Patriarch and the Synod of Constantinople.

3. One cannot pretend that these events were not what they were in that particularly troubled period of history. But now that today a more calm and equitable judgment has been brought to bear on them, it is important to recognize the excesses with which they were tainted and later led to consequences which, as far as we can judge, went much further than their authors had intended or expected. Their censures were aimed at

the persons concerned and not the churches; they were not meant to break ecclesiastical communion between the sees of Rome and Constantinople.

4. This is why Pope Paul VI and Patriarch Athenagoras I with his synod, certain that they are expressing the common desire for justice and the unanimous sentiment of charity on the part of their faithful, and remembering the command of the Lord: "If you are offering your gift at the altar, and there remember that your brother has something against you, leave your gift before the altar and go first to be reconciled to your brother" (Matt. 5:23-24), declare with one accord that:

a) They regret the offensive words, the reproaches without foundation and the reprehensible gestures which on both sides marked and accompanied the sad events of that period;

b) They also regret and wish to erase from the memory and midst of the church the sentences of excommunication which followed them, and whose memory has acted as an obstacle to a rapprochement in charity down to our own day, and to consign them to oblivion;

c) Finally they deplore the troublesome precedents and the later events which, under the influence of various factors, among them lack of understanding and mutual hostility, eventually led to the effective rupture of ecclesiastical communion.

5. This reciprocal act of justice and forgiveness, as Pope Paul VI and Patriarch Athenagoras I with his synod are aware, cannot suffice to put an end to the differences, ancient or more recent, which remain between the Roman Catholic Church and the Orthodox Church and which, by the action of the Holy Spirit, will be overcome, thanks to the purification of hearts, regret for historical errors and an effective determination to arrive at a common understanding and expression of the apostolic faith and its demands.

In accomplishing this act, however, they hope that it will be pleasing to God, who is prompt to pardon us when we forgive each other, and recognized by the whole Christian world, but especially by the Roman Catholic Church and the Orthodox Church together, as the expression of a sincere mutual desire for reconciliation and as an invitation to pursue, in a spirit of mutual trust, esteem and charity, the dialogue which will lead them, with the help of God, to live once again for the greater good of souls and the coming of the kingdom of God, in the full communion of faith, brotherly concord and of a sacramental life which existed between them throughout the first millennium of the life of the church.

II. Statement by Middle Eastern Church Leaders

This is excerpted from a statement signed by four Middle Eastern church leaders following a meeting at the Amba Bishoy monastery in Egypt in November 1987. Those signing the statement were Pope Shenouda III, Patriarch of the Coptic Orthodox Church, Parthenios III, Greek Orthodox Patriarch of Alexandria and All Africa, Karekin II, Catholicos of the Armenian Apostolic Church (Cilicia) and Ignatius IV, Greek Orthodox Patriarch of Antioch and All the East.

While reflecting once more on the deeply rooted inner unity of faith existing among our two families of churches, we rejoice in realizing how much we have advanced in our rediscovery and in the growing consciousness among our people of that inner unity of faith in the Incarnate Lord.

Attempts by theologians of both families aimed at overcoming the misunderstandings inherited from the past centuries of alienation towards one another have happily reached the same conclusion that fundamentally and essentially we on both sides have preserved the same faith in our Lord Jesus Christ, in spite of diverse formulations and resulting controversies...

We affirm our togetherness in the true understanding of the person of Christ, who being God of God, the only begotten Son of the Father, became truly man, fully assumed our human nature without losing or diminishing or changing his divine nature. Being perfect God, he became perfect man without confusion, without separation.

In the light of this conviction, we recommend that the official dialogue on both regional [Middle East] and international levels be pursued through common endeavours in the healthy process of clarifying and enhancing our commonness in faith and dispelling the misapprehensions of the past, thus preparing the way towards the full recovery of our communion.

We urge our people to continue to deepen their consciousness in the deep commonality of faith and to relate to one another as brethren and sisters who share the same gospel, the same faith and the same commission entrusted to them by their common Lord.

Thanks be to God that ancient controversies and rivalries have given way to a new era of sincere and open dialogue and communal brotherhood. We pray that these most difficult and crucial times in the Middle East may stimulate all of us to see more clearly the demand the command of our Lord Jesus Christ so that we may be one according to his will (John 10) and prayer (John 17).

III. WCC-Orthodox Relations

The following is excerpted from comments by WCC General Secretary Emilio Castro and Dimitrios I, Ecumenical Patriarch of Constantinople, during their meeting at the Ecumenical Centre in Geneva in December 1987.

It really is a unique privilege for the WCC to have within it all the Orthodox churches. This has been possible because of the determination — we may well say the *historic* determination — of the Ecumenical Patriarchate, which as early as 1920 called upon all the churches to establish a *koinonia* of all Christians, dedicated to the service of all humanity and to an undivided peace that would know no frontiers.

In 1948 the Ecumenical Patriarchate was among the founders of the WCC. Since then, your holy church has been carrying out a model ecumenical ministry, drawing other churches into the movement of unity, a unity built on the faith that the church of Christ is a unique, indivisible unity and that Christ is Lord of all.

The presence of Orthodoxy in this movement is at once real and symbolic. For your example has taught us that we are incomplete in our own universality when we live in alienation from the others. Our catholicity is diminished and incomplete so long as we remain shut up within our own individual or confessional walls. Division and alienation prevent us from living out the full mystery of catholicity.

The ecumenical movement has likewise taught us that all churches have a share of responsibility in the history of separation and schism. Being aware of this, we must therefore overturn the barriers which have broken up the universality of the church and must look for immediate and long-term ways of common witness and service. Since we pray "for universal peace, for the well-being of the holy churches of God and for all to be one", we ourselves must constantly be one...

One of the things the ecumenical movement has learned is that there cannot be any universal church without Orthodoxy. The ecumenical movement has been showing an increasing interest in the tradition of the Orthodox churches, their ecclesiology and their spirituality as these have been lived out through a long and arduous history. But this interest is not merely historical and confessional in its scope.

The Orthodox presence in the quest for the visible unity of all Christians is of itself full of ecumenical significance. For Orthodoxy brings with it the passion for the unity of the church of the first millennium, the liturgical dimension in the Christian life, the vision of a coherent, organic ecumenism, the sense that it is the Spirit of God who is himself guiding and leading us into the kingdom of God.

The doctrinal and liturgical tradition of Orthodoxy is the oldest and most authentic form of a tradition at once apostolic and ecumenical. Orthodoxy is a world of great riches...

Emilio Castro

The Ecumenical Patriarchate has been keen on the ecumenical idea right from the start, and has always considered it — like all related activities inspired by it — the most positive beginning and most helpful means for bringing the churches together, for achieving their coexistence, collaboration and common development, and for their common progress towards the accomplishment of their final, visible Christian union...

Up to this day, [the WCC] has placed itself at the disposal of all the churches and denominations which confess Jesus Christ as God and Saviour, and which have responded to the call to visible unity in the world, to the glory of the Triune God...

We can unreservedly say that the WCC enjoys due recognition and deep respect from us. Consequently, we reiterate our conviction... that the Orthodox presence in the Council should be seen as a normal phenomenon, both indispensable and useful in many ways.

The ecclesiological self-awareness of the Orthodox Church means that it sees the longed-for unity of the churches as a gift of Christ, really present in Orthodoxy as it lives the reality of the one, holy, catholic and apostolic church. For us, there is no doubt that this is the model to be used in the search for unity.

We know that there have been genuine instances in the Council where, repeatedly and from the very start, this point has been stressed... At the same time, we hope that, in the near future..., this Orthodox presence may, in helping to achieve the Council's aims, grow ever stronger and more representative in its personnel, in its potential and in the contributions it makes both theologically and in spirituality...

[The WCC's] study programmes, theological and otherwise, and its various activities in very many fields of joint Christian witness and service are truly most positive elements. In this, if in no other way, the hopeful reality is affirmed whereby, even if the desired full unity of the churches on a purely ecclesiological and theological level is not assured, it is nevertheless possible to act together in the service of modern man in the most pressing and urgent issues of his life. We feel that this in itself is an important victory for the ecumenism which we, as a church, are cultivating...

We rejoice in the coexistence of this Council's member churches under the same roof, as they search for the direct ways to unity granted by the Lord... We also rejoice because, as Orthodox, we find beneath this roof the possibility of witnessing to the faith and teaching we have received — a witness we consider and carry out as a humble service to the Lord's will.

Dimitrios I